# Stop fat dead in its tracks!

In these pages, Shirley Cook teaches you how to commit *Murder on the FAT Express*. With the sword of the Lord, you can eliminate those villains who have been sabotaging your diet plans. *Murder on the FAT Express* gives you a five-part plan of attack:

- *Evidence* — revealing tongue-in-cheek vignettes of the author's battle with overweight
- *Hey, Partner*—confronting the truths of obesity
- *Clue*—An upbeat little poem to confirm your stand against fat
- *Diet Data*—great tips and recipe strategies
- *Solution* — An inspiring biblical verse to remind you that you can bump off those bumps and lumps with the Lord's help!

By Shirley Cook

*The Exodus Diet Plan*
*Murder on the FAT Express*

# MURDER ON THE FAT EXPRESS

## SHIRLEY COOK

**Power Books**

Fleming H. Revell
Old Tappan, New Jersey

Unless otherwise identified, Scripture quotations in this publication are from the Holy Bible, New International Version. Copyright © 1973, 1978, 1984 International Bible Society. Used by permission of Zondervan Bible Publishers.

Scripture quotations identified KJV are from the King James Version of the Bible.

Library of Congress Cataloging-in-Publication Data

Cook, Shirley.
   Murder on the Fat Express / Shirley Cook.
     p.   cm.
   ISBN 0-8007-5349-6
   1. Reducing—Psychological aspects.   2. Self-
control.   I. Title.
   RM222.C66   1990
   613.2′5—dc20                       89-48623
                                                       CIP

Copyright © 1990 by Shirley Cook
Published by the Fleming H. Revell Company
Old Tappan, New Jersey 07675
Printed in the United States of America

# Contents

Contents

# MURDER ON THE FAT EXPRESS

# I Love a Mystery

How do you feel about mysteries? Do you watch them on TV? Do you check your favorite mystery writer's books out of the library? I do. And maybe you do, too, because you like to try your hand—and mind—at problem-solving.

Well, we have a mystery on our hands (and thighs) that sometimes seems unsolvable. This roll of fat around the waist—how did it get there? The lumps and bumps on our hips are not bruises, are they? And how about those heavy jowls? Surely they would look better on a linebacker or a bulldog than on you and me. How did we get this way? How can we lose weight without losing our minds? How can we solve this problem once and for all?

*Murder on the FAT Express* presents some mysteries and some solutions, but the final solution to the FAT problem rests with you—the detective. Whether you see yourself as a Jessica Fletcher, a Nancy Drew, or a Sherlock Holmes, you can and will solve the mystery of overweight as you read and apply the precepts presented in this book.

The "Evidence" will encourage and amuse you, and the "Solutions" will inspire and fortify you. But the most powerful tool in this book will be your own personal detective work in completing the questionnaire at the end of each entry. You can discover the key that will unlock the mystery of your compulsive eating as you honestly reach into yourself and record what you uncover. You don't have to be a victim any longer! As you write your deepest feelings (keep the book as you would a diary—for your eyes only), you will commit *Murder on the FAT Express*.

Be patient with yourself. It took months, maybe even years, to get out of shape, so it will take time to become trim and fit. You may read through the book several times, and each time you reread your own insights, you will learn something new. Again I say, be patient. Our bodies come to us as a gift from God, and they deserve special love and care—and patience.

If you're like me, you've probably tried every diet out there. Let's not think *diet* this time; let's just *do it*. Choose a food plan (preferably one approved by your doctor), then begin to live it—one meal at a time—one day at a time—one pound at a time. Together, with the Lord's help, we can break the pound barrier. Forever!

So come along, partner. Let's commit ourselves to each other and to God. I love a mystery!

> And he made known to us the mystery of his will according to his good pleasure, which he purposed in Christ, to be put into effect when the times will have reached their fulfillment—to bring all things in heaven and on earth together under one head, even Christ.
>
> Ephesians 1:9, 10

## **Self-Evaluation Quiz**

My name.


My approximate height and weight.


My favorite foods

My favorite books.



Am I a doer or a watcher? Explain.



My favorite clothes.



What do I think of my appearance?



What are my feelings about myself?

Do I have any goals? What are they?

Would weight loss improve my quality of life? Why? Why not?

Am I willing to make a positive change in my eating habits? If yes, sign and date this page.

Signature_____Date_____

# It's a Mystery to Me!
## (Fat—Again?)

### Evidence:

It was a dark and stormy night. . . .

Actually, it was a bright, sunny morning on a recent trip to Hawaii—a business trip for my husband, Les, and a vacation for me. I dragged myself out of bed, pulled the cord of the typical Hilton Hotel draperies, and stared in wonder at the sight below. Waikiki Beach. White sand. Blue water. Pink, green, and purple bikinis.

I ran to my suitcase, pulled out my one-piece swimsuit, and dashed into the bathroom to get ready for my debut. It had been months—okay, years—since I had worn the flowery orange-and-brown, slightly out-of-date bathing suit, but I didn't give it a thought until I began to tug and pull at the faded polyester rag. Had it shrunk? It was not only narrower than I remembered but shorter as well. I puffed and panted while tucking dimpled pads of cellulite into the brown fabric.

I winced as the straps settled down in the grooves of my rounded shoulders, and the legs tightened around my thighs like a tourniquet. It was then I remembered a quotation by Orson Welles: "Gluttony is not a secret vice."

I tiptoed from the bathroom to look at my reflection in the full-length mirror on the closet door. There, to my horror, was a Kewpie stuffed into a Barbie Doll swimsuit.

As I rolled the offending garment into a ball and hid it under a bigger-than-life sweatshirt, I realized I had a mystery on my hands. And my thighs. And my hips. How did I get so fat—again? I've been on diets. I've even written diet books. How embarrassing! I glanced over my shoulder at the mirror. Had anyone else noticed?

## Hey, Partner:

Have you looked in a full-length mirror lately? You may have observed that you don't have to worry about watching your waistline—because it's right out there in front of you.

I was really depressed that morning in Honolulu. I didn't join my friends at the beach because I was too humiliated to parade that white flesh in front of them. Instead, I hid myself under long pants and an oversize shirt. How are you hiding today?

You can continue to lie to yourself: "I'm not *that* fat; I don't care how I look; fat people are jolly; I love to eat more than I love to feel thin." Or you can come into partnership with me. We'll be our own detective agency and pursue this mystery of excess pounds. Our case will be to find a workable solution to fat, and day by day put to death the old self-destructive nature.

# Clue:

If moderation is a virtue
And gluttony is a sin,
Then I really have a choice
To be either fat or thin!

# Diet Data:

At breakfast eat like a king—you will use most of your energy in the early hours of the day. At lunch eat like a prince—you won't suffer from drowsiness. At dinner eat like a pauper—you'll sleep better and lose weight faster.

# Solution:

Do not join those who drink too much wine
    or gorge themselves on meat,
for drunkards and gluttons become poor,
    and drowsiness clothes them in rags.

Proverbs 23:20, 21

Do I feel self-conscious about my weight?

Have I succeeded or failed at dieting?

Do I hide my overweight by clothes or action? How?

Do I really believe I can conquer my overeating habit? How?

Do I think I can control my food intake by myself, or do I need God's help and strength? Explain.

My own thoughts about the Scripture verse in today's Solution.

# Undercover Agent

## (Honesty)

## Evidence:

The fragrance of tropical flowers lingered in the night air as soft breezes rustled the overhanging palms. Water lapped at the shoreline, and I dug my bare toes into the warm sand as Les and I strolled along, hand in hand.

"Where did you get that?" My husband's eyes swept over my ankle-length flowered dress.

"It's a muumuu. All the women wear them."

I let out a long sigh. Boy, I sure was comfortable. No constraining waistbands. Just free-flowing everything. I didn't have to hold my stomach in or give those bulges a thought. I had gone undercover.

After several minutes, I blurted, "Honey, do you think I'm fat?"

Les's eyes shifted uncomfortably. "Hmm, I wouldn't say you're exactly *fat*."

I felt the hair on the back of my neck bristle. "Well, what *exactly* would you say?"

A cold breeze blew between us. "Do we have to talk about this tonight?"

Tears stung my eyes, but I forced a laugh. "Of course not. Say, I know what I'd like." As the moon hid behind a cloud, my feelings slipped behind a wall of cheerfulness. "Let's get an ice-cream cone—one of those chocolate macadamia-nut kind."

As I licked the cold, creamy smoothness, my muscles relaxed. Why did I feel so angry? I had thrown Les a loaded question. But he should have answered differently. He should have told me I wasn't fat. He should have. . . .

After we turned out the lights, I lay in bed wide awake. Did it really matter if I was overweight? Some of the most beautiful women I know are soft and round. Even the TV stars are getting plump. I smiled to myself. That Roseanne was a kick! And how about Barbara Bush? Not overweight, but not a twig either. A real elegant lady. I knew in my heart that God was not in the least concerned about size. He loves us all equally, regardless of color, creed, age, or weight. True, I had gained twenty pounds in three years, and it was also true that, if I continued to gain at that rate, in ten years I would weigh over two hundred pounds!

I tossed and turned, trying to decide if I was obsessed by pride or anger. Was it Les's fault I was so miserable? Did the blame belong on my children? My circumstances? My genes?

*Face it*, I heard an inner voice say. *Confess. You did this to yourself. Fat is not the real problem. It is the obvious result of hidden feelings—emotions you've been afraid to face.*

I sat bolt upright in bed, threw off the blanket, and ran to the mirror. The moon filtered through the window, illuminating a hazy reflection. "That's it!" I said aloud. "I don't have to be fat. I just need to understand why I keep hiding behind a wall of flesh."

"What's wrong?" came a sleepy voice from the bed.

"Nothing," I said, crawling back into bed. "I've just decided to come out from undercover."

"Hmm, that's good," Les mumbled. "It is kind of hot in here."

## Hey, Partner:

We can't get over our food addiction until we're honest about it. Blaming others only adds more calories to the corpus. There's a way to solve this mystery, but we have to be willing to interrogate ourselves, then face the charges.

It took me more than three years to finally "fess up" to my own denial. I didn't want to admit I used food to soothe my hurt feelings and bolster my sagging ego. But I can see now that I have to take control of my own eating habits. No pleading the Fifth Amendment. God will give wisdom along with self-control, the fruit of the Spirit, as we trust in Him. "Read me my rights!"

## Clue:

> I will confess to Him,
> I will agree with God
> That gluttony is a sin
> That can truly ruin my "bod."

## Diet Data:

Try fasting every day from 9:00 P.M. until bedtime. Food eaten while watching the late show shows up early on the waistline.

23

## Solution:

"Then you will know the truth, and the truth will set you free." . . . Jesus replied, "I tell you the truth, everyone who sins is a slave to sin . . . if the Son sets you free, you will be free indeed."

John 8:32, 34, 36

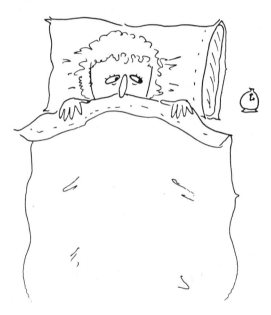

Is it difficult for me to handle strong emotions? Why?

How do I respond when I feel angry?

Whose "fault" is it that I am overweight?

How did my parents contribute to my problem of overeating?

Am I obsessed with food?

Throughout the day, how often do I think of food?

Why is it difficult to admit my food addiction?

How can being truthful about my overeating set me free?

Who spoke the words in today's Solution? Did He speak the truth?

# The Plot Thickens
## (Denial)

## Evidence:

The voice in the night, the tug at my undercover operations—both were left behind on that island paradise. I didn't want to face another diet. Hadn't I tried them all—and failed?

There was the "Water Diet" I'm sure caused the shortage of '76; the "Citrus Diet" which did no more than twist my lips into a continuous pucker; and the infamous "Prune Pit Diet." That one kept me sucking pits until I asked my husband if he noticed a difference in me. He answered, "Yes, you look different, all right. You look like a squirrel trying to find a place to hide his acorns!"

I won't say I didn't lose weight on any of those countless diets. The problem was that, after each major weight loss, I promptly gained back the pounds plus five more. I was convinced that diets don't work—at least not for me.

After I returned home from Hawaii, I fell into my old routine of countless peanut-butter-and-cracker breaks and late-night eating. As the mystery of the hidden calories grew, so did I. As much as I wanted to deny I had a food addiction, the day of judgment approached all too quickly. Other voices spoke, this time not in the dark but right out in broad daylight!

1. Good Friend: "My husband mentioned that you look as if you've put on some weight." *Ouch.*
2. Parent: "You've put on a few pounds since I saw you last year, honey." *Oooh.*
3. Daughter: "Hey, Mom, the seam in your sweatpants has split open." *Oh, no!*
4. Husband: "Who ate all the peanut butter?" *Moi?*

I love and trust my friends and family, but were they suggesting I go on another diet? The plot thickens—along with my waistline and ankles.

It was truth time, and I had not only to face the truth but to embrace it wholeheartedly as well. Only then would I be set free from my own denial.

# Hey, Partner:

Have you noticed that the moment you decide to take control of your eating monster, something inside your head "clicks"? Could that be the sound of a key turning in your shackles?

That's what happened to me. The belief that I was to be forever shut up in a prison of fat seemed to fall away. I knew that "nothing is impossible with God" (Luke 1:37), and that He would lead me down the long, dark corridor of my own fears to bring me into the freedom of "lightness." Today can be your day of release, too. Once we lay aside our denial that we are in bondage to food, we will find God is present to show us the way out—one step at a time.

Trust Him.

Trust yourself.

You deserve the good feelings that come from a controlled appetite and a healthy body.

# Clue:

Fear of failure is a trap
That holds me in its grip.
So I must hand myself a slap
To give my fears the slip!

# Diet Data:

Instead of following those crazy diets, plan your weight management to include new and interesting low-cal recipes. Learn ten new ones to implement your weight-loss plan. Different spices jazz up old recipes. Salsa is an excellent addition. There are also some butter-flavored powders that include sour cream in the taste.

# Solution:

So do not fear, for I am with you;
do not be dismayed, for I am your God.
I will strengthen you and help you;
I will uphold you with my righteous right hand.

Isaiah 41:10

Am I fat? Write a sentence admitting the truth.

My decision to take control of my eating monster.

My statement of faith that with God nothing is impossible.

The Plot Thickens (Denial)

I believe I deserve a healthy body because:

List the diets I have tried and state why I did not maintain the weight loss.

# Murder on the FAT Express

## (Day of Decision)

## Evidence:

"I say that *Professor Plum* committed the murder in the kitchen with the knife."

My youngest daughter, Barby, and I used to play Clue by the hour. I never won. I always ended up in the kitchen with the knife. Just try to tell me I'm not drawn to that warm, friendly place where cookies and pies are born.

My home centers around the kitchen—literally. In the front door, through the kitchen, to the family room. To reach a comfortable place to sit down, you have to pass the refrigerator and cupboards, so why relax without something to munch on?

That room of tempting goodies needs a bypass, and so will I if I don't get out a sharp knife and cut away calories—especially FAT calories. I've come to the conclusion that my overeating strongly resembles the addiction drug and alcohol abusers face, for my life seems to revolve around food.

I don't remember what the bride wore at a formal wedding, but the prime rib and pasta served at the reception sticks in my mind—and other places. Could I tell you if Betty had a baby girl or boy? No, but the cake covered with pink whipped cream was yummy. Then there are the many business trips when I accompany Les. Do I recall anything about the French Quarter of New Orleans other than the Cajun food and beignets? Our sojourns to Florida are memorable to me because of the taste of stone crab; the excursions to Sonoma Valley are culinary treats of fresh French bread, sharp cheddar cheese, and steamy cups of espresso coffee.

I have visited restaurants and hotels in Yosemite Valley, Point Reyes Peninsula, and even China and have used research information for books I've written. So all is not lost on my appetite. (Honestly, my love for Chinese food was not my primary purpose for going there!) But now it's time to write a new chapter in my book of life: *Murder on the FAT Express.*

I need a weight-management program. No diets, please, that will take me into the next stage of life without the burden of love handles or thighs competing to pass each other. The quick-loss diets are out. No more cloak-and-dagger games for me.

"Just the facts, ma'am. Just the facts."

# Hey, Partner:

"You have the right to remain silent," or you can speak up for yourself. To be a silent partner in this thinness project can be our undoing. We need to say how we feel about our over-eating. We need to tell it like it is: "I am overweight. I got this way by overeating."

The facts.

The Apostle Paul wrote in Romans 10:9, "If you confess with your mouth, 'Jesus is Lord,' and believe in your heart that God raised him from the dead, you will be saved."

The facts.

Confession of our belief in Christ will bring about the miracle of new birth into God's family. There you and I can enjoy not only the companionship of the Lord Jesus Christ but we can also have the sure hope of eternal life after these bodies cease to function.

Have you made that decision to turn your past, present, and future over to God? If not, today is the day you can experience a peace and joy you thought impossible. After that first life-changing decision, each step along the rocky road of life is taken with continuing belief and confession. I met Christ as my Lord and Savior when I was twenty-one years old, and though I have disappointed Him many times, He has never let me down.

Today, I make a fresh confession: "I got myself into this shape, and with God's help and direction, I will get myself into a new, healthy shape."

## Clue:

To murder FAT is my goal,
A case of do or die.
My decision comes from the soul,
And my lips do not lie!

## Diet Data:

Don't make your final goal the only goal, or you'll become discouraged. Plan a reward after every five-pound loss, and increase the value with each milestone. New earrings in the beginning. Maybe a blouse or skirt after the next goal. By the time you reach your ideal weight, you'll have a wardrobe with pizzazz in it.

## Solution:

Do not lie to each other, since you have taken off your old self with its practices and have put on the new self, which is being renewed in knowledge in the image of its Creator.

Colossians 3:9, 10

In what way is my food addiction similar to that of an alcoholic?

Am I willing to admit my addiction to someone?

The person I will "confess" to is:

Have I believed in Jesus Christ as my own Savior and Lord?

Did I confess to someone that I believe in Jesus?

Who knows I am a believer?

When and where did I trust Christ as Savior?

I have never trusted in Christ before, but today I turn my life over to Him.
I will tell＿＿＿＿＿＿＿that I now believe in Christ.

The Solution states that I am being renewed in whose image?

# Modus Operandi
## (Plan of Attack)

## Evidence:

Now that I've been found out, I have to face the music. To lose weight, I must release more calories than I take in, and to keep the pounds off, I'll have to continue the balance of energy in/energy out. This looks like a life-style change to me.

I read recently that unless you want to continue a weight-management plan for the rest of your life, it is better not to start one. The writer went on to say that 95 percent of the people who try to lose weight either never reach their goal or, if they do, they are unable to maintain the weight loss. Only one in twenty dieters continues in his success. The yo-yo syndrome is not only detrimental to health but also to self-esteem. Don't I know it!

I have made the decision to take control of my eating habits, but now there is another decision lurking in the shadows.

Shall I attempt to capture the culprit on my own, or do I enlist a backup? A group? Should I go for the freeze-dried food or learn good nutrition and food preparation? As I said before, I've already tried the fad diets, so that's out, but there are many really good programs to choose from.

One friend recently joined a group that weighs her several times a week and offers food (for sale, of course) in convenient freeze-dried packets. She said, "This stuff tastes like it looks. Cardboard delights!" But she is losing weight and likes the program because she's single, busy, and doesn't have time to worry about or prepare meals.

Joanna attends a weekly "anonymous" meeting. She finds the members helpful and supportive and is free to devise her own eating plan. Bertie enjoys receiving little prizes and rewards from her weight-loss group. She was even crowned queen. Another friend relies on a Christian support group that counts calories and prays for one another. Then there's Meg (and Oprah), who lost with a medically supervised liquid diet.

Although I'm confused, I'm also glad there are so many options. But which "M.O." fits my temperament—and my checkbook? And which one can I live with until I reach the end of the road?

I know I need accountability, so going it on my own won't do for me. I also need to weigh in each week, find support from others who are learning self-control, and I could use a pep talk from a winner!

With all those requirements, I decided to return to the organization that helped me ten years ago. It wasn't their fault I was a yo-yo. The program is worldwide and rates number one nutritionally and motivationally. Besides, I could end up looking like Lynn Redgrave!

Come Saturday morning I will step out of my "gumshoes" and onto the scale. Oooh, am I sure I want to do this?

# Hey, Partner:

It isn't enough to admit we're fat. We have to plan the attack. Dieting (I use the word for lack of a better one) takes *desire, discipline,* and *determination.* No plan or group is enough without that 3-D vision. So if the *desire* for thinness is stronger than the desire for an extra helping of fat-laden food, we will *discipline* our out-of-control eating habits. The word *discipline* may have unpleasant connotations, but it really means, "training that produces obedience, self-control, or a particular skill." We need that training to carry out our resolve with *determination.*

I'm here to help you with a nudge of encouragement and even a smile or two. Together we can stake out the suspect— that overactive appetite—and with the orders and authority of our Commander, Jesus Christ, we will make our "collar."

# Clue:

> If it's weight you want to lose
> There are diet groups aplenty.
> It's just so hard to choose
> When there are more than twenty!
> > (So—some words are hard to rhyme.)

# Diet Data:

Apples (minus Alar, of course) are still good nutrition. They not only act as a diuretic but pectin, a natural water-soluble fiber found in apples, also helps delay digestion. Add an apple to your menu for greater satiety and weight loss.

## Solution:

"I know the plans I have for you," declares the Lord, "plans to prosper you and not to harm you, plans to give you hope and a future."

Jeremiah 29:11

Do I believe that if I find the "right" diet, I will succeed?

Was my inability to lose weight a result of my fear of weight loss?

How do I think my life will change if I lose weight?

What diet plan would best suit my personality and life-style?

Am I willing to spend time and effort to change my eating habits?

Is my goal to lose weight a short-term desire (class reunion, vacation, wedding)?

I am going to lose weight for which of the following: my partner, my parents, my friends, myself. Why?

I am going to lose weight because.

# The Shadow Knows
## (Fear of Failure)

## Evidence:

Dark clouds hung over the barren trees, threatening to unleash a winter storm. It was Saturday morning, the day of my first weigh-in and the beginning of a new life. But as I stared out the window (in the kitchen, of course), my resolve began to fade. Suppose I should fail—again? It had been more than ten years since I had begun and actually finished a weight-loss plan. I had started so many but never again reached that "ideal" goal.

I tugged at the straining buttons on my blouse. Maybe I shouldn't have eaten so much before going to bed last night. But I had to get rid of those chocolates. I didn't want to be tempted by them anymore. And there was the leftover Christmas fruitcake, hickory-smoked almonds, and that last smidgen of onion dip. What had I done? Added an extra three pounds, that's what!

There was no backing out. I had to face the scale. I had to take control of my own bad eating habits. "Lord," I prayed as I drove to the meeting place, "I've really blown it—into a balloon-shaped body. I don't have willpower, and I certainly don't have 'won't power,' but I can have Your power as I trust You. Help!"

"He who dwells in the shelter of the Most High will rest in the shadow of the Almighty" (Psalm 91:1).

The Shadow knows—and cares.

After I parked the car, I walked the short distance to the meeting place. The sun peeked through the clouds and smiled over my shoulder, casting a long, slim shadow in front of me. I glanced behind me. No one there! The shadow was attached to my feet and led me directly to the door.

This would be the new me. My shadow at noon would no doubt be realistically short and wide, but I planned to remember that tall, thin image as a prospect of the future. There was nothing to fear but my own doubts.

I lifted my chin(s), nodded a good-bye to my shadow, and walked through the door to join the happy, hopeful people inside.

# Hey, Partner:

Have you noticed that what we fear most usually fails to materialize? Take the fear of weight gain. We are afraid we'll fail another diet and eventually pop more buttons, or possibly an artery or two. We even fear weight loss.

Success at the scale is an unknown. Will the people who know me as a fat friend reject the new me? Suppose I become so glamorous and irresistible that Hollywood comes pounding on my door! My friends will be jealous; my mate will feel threatened.

Come on. Let's get real. Most of us are just average folks, with average looks at best. We are not learning new eating habits to keep from ballooning or to gain stardom. We just want to be the best "me" we can possibly be. If our goal to lose weight contains the motive, "Once I'm thin, my life will be perfect," we are doomed to disappointment. Life may be much as it was before we slimmed down, with this exception: we will have discovered that we *can* be successful; we *can* complete what we begin; and we *are* worthwhile persons, deserving of our own approval.

Let's put aside our fears—all of them. We can abide one day at a time under the shadow of the Almighty. We are safe there.

## Clue:

> In my dreams I was skinny,
> But noontime sun brought alarm
> Because the shadow following me
> Was bigger than a barn.

## Diet Data:

Nonfat plain yogurt (the brand that rhymes with cannon) is a delicious substitute for mayonnaise and sour cream. It even makes a great topping for fruit.

## Solution:

> Keep me as the apple of your eye;
>    hide me in the shadow of your wings
> from the wicked who assail me,
>    from my mortal enemies who surround me.
>
> Psalm 17:8,9

Time to face the facts. List some significant times in my life that I began to put on weight (death in the family, job loss, divorce).

Did overeating solve my problems?

Does overeating ever take away loneliness, anger, fear? Why not?

Write down my difficulties in experiencing unwelcome emotions.

Am I afraid to feel conflict? Am I afraid to express it?

How can today's Solution be of greater help in dealing with my fears than an extra helping of ice cream?

# D.O.A.: Dead on Arrival
## (Positive/Negative Attitudes)

## Evidence:

"Do I have to starve to death just so I can live a little longer?"

"Just think how much sooner I could enjoy heaven if I didn't eat such nutritious food."

"By the time another meal rolls around, I'm already D.O.A.!"

These are only a few of the murmurings that have come out of my mouth through the years of dieting. No wonder I never made it to my goal. Imagine a marathon runner with more than twenty miles of track stretched before him. If he runs with that same negative attitude, his thoughts after the first mile might be, *Is it worth all this pain just to win a trophy?*

*Why am I out here running when I could drive this course in about a half an hour?*

*I'll probably die of ruptured blisters before I reach the finish line!*

That runner might as well turn in his Nikes for bedroom slippers, then head back to bed. And I might as well forfeit my new eating habits if I'm going to complain. I need the same positive attitude to lose weight as a runner needs to win a race.

Earlier, I mentioned an article in which a doctor said, "If you don't intend to change your diet and eating habits for life—don't bother to start. Yo-yo dieting CAN BE HAZARDOUS TO YOUR HEALTH." That's positive!

Sure, we're all going to die one day, but why not be as healthy as possible now so we can raise our quality of life? If changing the way I eat has an influence on my avoiding heart disease or cancer, it's worth the effort. I know there will be days when old habits will rear their ugly heads, but I'll face those days when they come. For now, I'm putting my negative attitudes away. The pounds may not disappear as quickly as I might wish, but that doesn't mean I won't reach my goal—someday.

Remember the story of the hare and the tortoise? The friend who loses five pounds a week for two or three weeks is like a sprinter who can't go long distances. She'll drop out of the race before the finish line is in sight. I know. That's the diet story of my life. This time—this last time—I'm putting on my tortoise shell and taking it slow and steady. I'll get there. Yes, I will.

## Hey, Partner:

It's really no mystery why we've regained lost weight or why we never complete a diet project. We don't need to do much sleuthing to uncover the answer. Come with me into the darkroom to look at the evidence.

Here is the film, ready to be developed. It portrays images—real-life images of you and me. We can see ourselves by holding the film up to the light, but in the negative state, we see the dark side of ourselves. This isn't the real "us." But when the negative is exposed to light for just the right amount of time, we will get a positive picture.

Our negative attitudes come from the darkness, not from the Light of the world. Satan's whispers are always negative: "You can't amount to anything. You are worthless. You aren't good enough to deserve God's favor."

We don't need to listen to those lies. The Lord Jesus Christ is Truth; He is Light. His word comes to us clearly:

"I have redeemed you; I have summoned you by name; you are mine" (Isaiah 43:1).

"Whatever your hand finds to do, do it with all your might . . ." (Ecclesiastes 9:10).

"As the Father has loved me, so have I loved you. Now remain in my love" (John 15:9).

Positive words.

Positive thoughts.

Positive power.

We will not be D.O.A., partner. We will be alive.

# Clue:

If you run, run as fast as you can,
You'll soon crumble, Gingerbread Man.
Instead be a tortoise; slow your pace,
And you will surely win the race.

## Diet Data:

Eat slower. Taste your food. Enjoy the texture. It takes twenty minutes for your mind to catch up with your stomach. A lot of damage can be done in those minutes.

## Solution:

> Finally, brothers, whatever is true, whatever is noble, whatever is right, whatever is pure, whatever is lovely, whatever is admirable—if anything is excellent or praiseworthy—think about such things. . . . And the God of peace will be with you.
>
> Philippians 4:8, 9b

My negative attitudes about myself.

My positive attitudes about myself.

My negative attitudes about my family.

My positive attitudes about my family.

My negative attitudes about my circumstances.

My positive attitudes about my circumstances.

My negative attitudes about God.




My positive attitudes about God.




Today I deliberately focus on my positive attitudes!
Today I deliberately thank God for all the good things in my life!

Signature_____Date_____

# Off Limits
## (Kick the Scale Habit)

### Evidence:

Many bad habits have contributed to my state of over-weight: peanut butter and crackers at bedtime; that extra slice of toast drizzled with honey; a hunk of cheese now and then when I'm feeling tired or bored; and a Snickers bar on each and every happy occasion. But I never dreamed that weighing myself daily, sometimes twice a day, could add to my weight gain.

Scenario: Yesterday I kept track of my food intake as well as my exercise output. I didn't add one thing to my plate that hadn't first been calorie-counted, measured, and tested for toxic waste. I even went to bed feeling a little hungry. This morning I brushed my teeth, washed my face, dropped my nightie, and boldly stepped onto the bathroom scale.

One pound! Lost? No. Gained. I felt terrible. I was a failure.

My heart began to beat erratically, my palms felt cold and moist, and my chin trembled. *Phooey.* All that misery for nothing. So what did I do? Did I quietly walk into the kitchen and begin another day of deprivation? No way. I ran to the cupboard, pulled out the cereal, that nutty-datey-sugary-granola type that I hid on the top shelf for company, and filled my favorite blue-and-white bowl to the top. I'd show 'em.

Oh, yeah? Who was I going to show? And what? The scale had won another battle over my determination to lose weight. I had given that one-eyed ogre undeserved power over me. I decided to let several days pass before I weighed myself again, so after breakfast, I settled back down to managing my food. For two days I avoided the scale. But I could hold out for only so long, you know.

Early Friday morning, I crept down the hall with a pen flashlight in my hand. Maybe if I sneaked up on the monster, I could catch it off guard. I edged around the corner, tiptoed across the cool linoleum, and gingerly balanced myself on the platform.

Two pounds! Gained? No. Lost. *Yippee!* I was a success.

I actually had lost two whole pounds in two days. I was ecstatic and immediately made plans to have lunch with a favorite friend at a favorite Mexican restaurant. The next day I again felt the call of the scale and discovered, to my horror, that those two pounds had ungraciously reappeared.

Failure. Success. Failure. Depression.

The scale is not a realistic measure of where I am weight-wise. Today I make the decision to weigh myself only once a week, and that primarily for the purpose of record keeping, not as a gauge of whether or not I am learning to manage food.

# Hey, Partner:

Did you know there are other ways to measure weight loss than stepping on a scale? How does your black skirt fit these days? Do you still have those little pads of fat caressing your jawbone? Touch your stomach. Does it really feel empty, or does the clock tell you when it's time to eat?

Until we can learn to listen to and be aware of our own bodies, we will continue to lose the battle with the scale. The numbers pointed out by that dial give a false reading of who we are. Our self-worth should never be determined by a piece of machinery. God says that you and I are worthy of His eternal love. As we look into His Word and learn obedience, we will not only grow in awareness to our Creator but we also will begin to understand these marvelous bodies God has entrusted to us. We will learn to differentiate between emotional, spiritual, and physical hunger, and we'll meet our needs by eating, sleeping, calling a friend, or spending time in prayer. It may take weeks, months, maybe even years, but we will see that weight management is really Life Management.

# Clue:

To measure success
You don't need a scale.
Jonah learned of his worth
From inside a whale.

# Diet Data:

Make a "Ten Most Wanted" list of your favorite low-calorie, low-fat foods and keep a good supply on hand.

## Solution:

The Lord abhors dishonest scales,
  but accurate weights are his delight.

Proverbs 11:1

How many times a week do I weigh myself?

How does the scale contribute to my feelings about myself?

Am I more concerned with numbers on a scale than I am of changed eating habits? Explain.

How could the scale be a detriment to my weight loss?

How can the scale be an encouragement in my weight loss?

How do I feel about myself when I see a gain at the scale?

How do I feel about myself when I see a loss at the scale?

Am I allowing the scale to control my innermost feelings?




List some other ways I can measure my commitment to food management.

# Trigger Happy
## (Danger Foods)

## Evidence:

Midnight. The house was quiet, except for the soft snoring sounds coming from our bedroom. I couldn't sleep, so I crept down the dark hallway, careful to avoid that squeaky board. I wouldn't want Les to know what I was doing. As cautiously as possible, I opened the door of the cabinet and peered inside. There it was on the shelf, behind several boxes. I felt the perspiration bead on my forehead as I contemplated taking it in my hand. My heart pounded so loudly I looked around to see if someone else had come into the room. Slowly my hand went toward the shiny object until I felt my fingers wrap around the cool surface. There was no backing out now. I clutched it to my chest, tightened my fingers around the hard surface—and ripped the seal off the plastic bag of corn chips!

My own personal trigger food had drawn me out of the safety of my bed into an eating binge. I curled up in a warm corner of the sofa and began to munch and crunch until more than half of the bag had disappeared—only to reappear in two days on my stomach and thighs. I had shot down my resolve by pulling the trigger on myself. I know that corn chips, tortilla chips—anything that resembles a taco—sends me over the border. The weight group I've joined calls this type of food "red light foods." And for good reason. I need to stop before putting these crunchy, salty tidbits into my mouth. I cannot eat just one. At least not now.

Corn chips are not the only food I have to be wary of. I love peanuts, peanut butter, almonds, macadamia nuts, and certain crackers. I can also be trigger happy over ice cream, cookies, and cheese. What weird shelf fellows! I know that one day I'll be able to eat these favorites in moderation, but for now, while I'm losing weight and learning self-control, I'll have to keep these items under lock and key. Better yet, I'll not even bring them home. To have these tempting foods in the house will only slow down my weight loss—and with every setback I feel my determination slip.

## Hey, Partner:

What are your "trigger happy" foods? We all have one or two, maybe more, foods that we can't leave alone after one bite. Now is a good time for you to identify yours. It is very unlikely that you binge on apples or spinach. As a rule, it's the fast food, the fat food, and the frozen food that pulls the trigger. If you have a penchant for cherry chocolates or candy bars, decide today that *for now* you will stay away from them. If even unpopped corn sets off your trigger, avoid it. *For now.*

I thought I'd be safe with microwave popcorn made for dieters, but I couldn't handle only one bag with no salt and butter. I popped all four bags, then buttered and salted them. I don't have popcorn in the house now; neither am I buying corn chips, but I've found an alternative to chips and salsa. Instead of those crunchy squares of salt and fat, I prepare a container of celery pieces, keep them in the refrigerator in cold water, and whenever I get the urge, I dish up my favorite salsa and happily munch away on my Mexican-style celery.

Instead of chocolate bars, I drink a cup of low-cal hot chocolate before going to bed; to replace my love of ice cream, I've substituted plain, nonfat yogurt flavored with frozen strawberries or crushed pineapple. And my rewards are coming. When I step on the scale each week, I not only discover I've lost some weight but I also find I've gained some good eating habits. Take time right now to identify your binge foods. Write them down and stick the list on the refrigerator door. Next to that piece of paper, list the foods you can temporarily substitute for your trigger foods. One day you'll be able to add those murderous delicacies back into your menu. Be patient. You will succeed this time. You will lose that unhealthy fat— and you will keep it off.

# Clue:

To avoid a food binge,
Recognize your trigger.
The fat will disappear,
The self-worth grow bigger.

# Diet Data:

A salad bar can be a disaster by the time a creamy dressing is slathered over those greens. With nonfat yogurt as a base, you can make your own creamy substitute. Add lemon juice, chopped onions, or cucumbers; garlic powder or mustard; or do as I do: add a seasonable amount of salsa.

## Solution:

> When tempted, no one should say, "God is tempting me." For God cannot be tempted by evil, nor does he tempt anyone; but each one is tempted when, by his own evil desire, he is dragged away and enticed.
>
> James 1:13, 14

What foods shoot down my weight-loss resolve?

How do sweet, creamy foods satisfy my emotional hunger?

How do crunchy foods relieve my emotional stress?

Does any type of food really touch me at a deep emotional level?

What am I trying to escape through eating?

What person(s) usually sets me off on an eating binge? Why?

Am I attempting to avoid what I consider unacceptable emotions?

Today I will admit and confront one of my hidden emotions (anger, envy, fear) by confessing it to God instead of swallowing it with food.

# The Lineup
## (Eating Types)

## Evidence:

When I was a teenager, I was asked to identify a man who was suspected of loitering and indecent exposure. I had seen enough detective movies to imagine the suspect, along with other criminal types, in a lineup. But for some reason, there were no others to line up. I stood in the same room, face-to-face with the man who had stopped me on the way to school to "ask directions." This man, the police told me, was an upstanding citizen, a member of the armed forces, and a respected husband and father. He wasn't the type to frighten young girls. But he was the man. Several other schoolmates were called in after I left, and each one identified him.

That was many years ago, but today I face another culprit in the lineup of eating types. What type of eater am I? Am I hungry midmorning? Midafternoon? Late at night? Do I prefer salty crunchies or cold creamies? To line up my eating type is important in this phase of my weight management if I want to succeed in the effort to reach my personal ideal weight.

In looking over my lineup, I've discovered that my emotions determine the type of food I reach for. When I feel lonely and in need of comfort, a big dish of ice cream soothes not only my sweet tooth but also my ruffled feelings. If I'm angry and unable to express my unhappiness, crunchy chips (lots of them) and spice seem to satisfy. Worry, anxiety, and frustration keep me grazing on whatever is available. Anything to calm the uneasiness. So how can I handle these eating moods?

First, I need to take a few minutes to look over the lineup before stuffing my face. I will ask myself if I am actually hungry or just restless. I want to know exactly what it is that's bothering me. Although food may, for a moment, quell my dissatisfaction, I can expect the placebo to wear off—and within minutes I will reach for more food.

Second, after knowing why I'm facing the open refrigerator, I will confess my need to God. He can comfort me in loneliness, soothe my anxieties, and fill my emotional void. He alone can meet the depths of my need.

Finally, I can plan what and when I will eat, whether it is something crunchy, cold, or creamy. I will wait twenty minutes for that food to register on my satiety index. My eating type is an extension of me that I can learn to acknowledge and work with. God is in control here—not my emotions.

## Hey, Partner:

How about joining me in the lineup? What type are you—the type to reach for the sweets? The salt? The solid? Don't put yourself down for your eating preferences; just learn how to manage them. Instead of filling a bowl with ice cream and chocolate fudge when you want something creamy, try a low-calorie milk shake you can whip up in your blender. All you need is some dry milk, cold water, ice cubes, and your favorite fruit. A little artificial sweetener will give you that sugary taste you love. For crunch, there are apples, celery, raw carrots, green peppers, even unbuttered popcorn (if that isn't a trigger food). Choose sweet or crunchy foods you can control. Give yourself plenty of time to eat, and enjoy the texture and flavor of whatever you've chosen to eat.

Our appetites are a God-given blessing to enable us to maintain healthy, strong bodies. Let's take the time to thank Him for His goodness. Then, as we eat, we can depend on Him to satisfy whatever need for food our bodies have. Beyond that, we look to the Lord to uncover and solve the real driving force behind our eating disorders.

I believe the secret of success in weight management is *knowing* when I am truly body-hungry, not emotion-hungry, and *learning* which foods, and how much, will satisfy that hunger. I'm not there yet, but I have hope for tomorrow while I live today.

# Clue:

> I'm not ashamed to stand
> In God's lineup today
> Because He has forgiven me
> And washed my sins away.

# Diet Data:

Instead of sautéing onions or other vegetables in fat, microwave them. Not only will they be softened but their flavor will be full-bodied as well. Put the veggies in a small cup and cover with vented plastic wrap. It only takes minutes and saves time at the stove and sink.

## Solution:

> Cast all your anxiety on him because he cares for you. Be self-controlled and alert. Your enemy the devil prowls around like a roaring lion looking for someone to devour.
>
> 1 Peter 5:7, 8

Who am I in the lineup of eating types?

What time of day am I most prone to overeat?

List some alternative actions to eating.

Am I afraid to experience hunger pangs? Why?

Does this fear revert to childhood memories? How?

Can I differentiate between *body hunger* and *appetite?*

Today I will allow myself to experience hunger for one full hour before I eat.

Write how I felt when my hunger pangs were ignored.

For one meal, I will take one-half the amount of my regular portion.

Did I feel anxious about eating less food?

# Gotcha!
## (Time Traps)

## Evidence:

Betsy says her time trap is set somewhere between lunch and dinner. She's tired and hungry after a long day of work, and after kicking off her shoes, she wants something to eat before preparing dinner for her family.

Audrey doesn't eat much breakfast, so her time trap opens up midmorning after she has spent several hours at her desk.

I've had urges at those times of the day, but my greatest trap comes at night, around nine o'clock. If I've decided to fast from nine until breakfast, I can manage to fall into the trap around 8:30 P.M. and busily fill up my tank until the clock strikes nine.

Just as there are early and late risers (often called morning or night people), there are also different times of the day that we have greater difficulty controlling our overeating. I think it has something to do with our body rhythms, the ebb and flow of our energy levels. For some, the days and nights go smoothly—until Saturday morning. Then suddenly, there's a click and the trap opens to bare its ugly teeth throughout the weekend.

What can we do to avoid these traps—ignore them? Hope they'll go away? No, we need to face them without stepping into their clutches. We can turn these times into positive and productive occasions.

In the months I've been learning weight-management skills, I have accomplished more around my house than I had in years. I channeled my energies into worthwhile projects that took me out of the kitchen: one month, I painted and papered my bedroom and bathroom; as the weather warmed, I took myself outside to turn the soil and plant wildflower gardens. I've cleaned the garage and the closets and still found time to read a couple of books and write several chapters of my novel.

There are things to do besides eat! In the process of finding projects, I am burning calories and making my home a more pleasant place to live. I have a list of things to do now when I feel the urge to return to my time trap.

Well, I'm kind of tired now, but not sleepy enough to go to bed. Hmmm, I wonder what might be good to eat. Whoops! Where's that list? Ah, yes. Now is a good time for me to settle down into a bubble bath and read that short story in my favorite magazine.

## Hey, Partner:

If your time trap is set to go off in the morning, you're in luck. You can always get outside for a walk, clean out some drawers, or bury yourself in those papers on your desk. If, like Betsy, your trap opens up before dinner, do as she does: sit down with a fresh cup of coffee, put up your feet, and just relax. After dark, your time trap can be diverted by picking up some knitting, working out to an exercise tape, or sinking up to your neck in a tub of scented water. Take a few minutes right now to honestly and objectively discover your own time traps—those times when you want to eat but know you shouldn't. Find some alternatives to eating. I've given you a few ideas, but you're smart enough to pick up this book, so I know you'll come up with some great thoughts of your own. You might even want to pass a few along to me and others who are trying to learn some lifetime habits for weight control.

I've saved my favorite idea for last because I hope you'll remember it best and try it first.

When my time trap rears its head, I bow mine. What better time to pray, to beseech my Lord, than when I am tempted to make food my god? Food doesn't provide love—God does. Food doesn't calm my restlessness—God does. When I want to reach for unnecessary food, I can pray for those who have none. Our Lord is always present, always sufficient, always sovereign. Let's begin to use our time traps to step out of time into eternity.

# Clue:

> Scrub the floor or take a bath;
> Which shall it be?
> Pine scent or jasmine;
> The choice is up to me.

# Diet Data:

Don't try to change all your behavior patterns at once, or you will become discouraged. Try one new change a week. For example: for one week, don't eat in front of the TV. The following week, eat only at the table. Next, you may want to limit yourself to only one helping instead of two. As you get one area under control, the next will come easier.

# Solution:

> But I trust in you, O Lord;
>   I say, "You are my God."
> My times are in your hands;
>   deliver me from my enemies
>   and from those who pursue me.

Psalm 31:14, 15

How does the time of day affect my appetite?

Am I most hungry when I'm tired or rested? Why?

Do I automatically reach for food when I sit down to relax?

Why do I think food plays such an important part in my life?

Do the food commercials on TV send me to the refrigerator?

What positive action will I take when such commercials flash on the screen?

I will purchase the following low-cal foods to have on hand when I am caught in a time trap.

I will not only have low-cal foods on hand but I also will eat them instead of rich food.

# Book 'im!
## (Food Diary)

## Evidence:

"Whatcha eatin', sweetie?

"Nuttin, honey."

"Sure sounds like you're over there chewing on something."

I glanced over my shoulder. If my husband could hear so well, why did he turn the TV on so loud? Besides, I was only finishing up a leftover taco. Surely it didn't matter. I was standing by the sink, after all. It wasn't even worth mentioning or writing in my food diary.

"Say," Les called to me later in the day, "what's this bag behind the couch?"

"Nuttin', honey!" I snatched the small brown sack in which I'd hidden the telltale candy wrappers from the night before. "I forgot to clean up after the kids had their friends over."

*Oooh.* I cringed at my quick lies before dashing out of the room with the wadded paper in my hand. My husband was no help at all. He made me feel guilty.

"You go to your weight group tomorrow, don't you?" His

tender look softened the words. "I'm sure proud of you, sweetie. I know how hard it must be to lose weight."

Would he be proud if he knew how many times I had cheated this week? Would I be proud when I joined the other dieters, knowing I had failed to keep my commitment? I was not only lying to my husband, my companions, and myself, but I was lying to the Lord as well. I was that double-minded person the Apostle James wrote about: unstable in all my ways.

I opened my spiral notebook where I kept track of the food I ate each day. There were days without a single recorded item. The days I ate the most, I wrote the least. I made excuses for myself: food eaten at the counter didn't count, and snacks eaten while watching a show wouldn't show. *Ha.*

The next day when I attended my weight group, the lecturer's talk was about the importance of recording the food we eat. Coincidence? I knew what she said was true, not only because I had gained weight that week but also because it is a good exercise in honesty. I'll think twice before grabbing a cookie. I know I'm going to record it, then subtract the calories from food I could enjoy later in the day. I will begin to plan what and when I eat throughout the day instead of allowing my greed and compulsion to guide me.

I plan which freeways to take to reach an unfamiliar destination; I plan how I will stretch the money to pay bills and have enough left over for Christmas gifts; I plan parties, picnics, and potlucks—why not plan my daily dinners? And lunches? And breakfasts? I'll lose weight and stay healthier when my plans include my body's daily nutritional requirements.

# Hey, Partner:

A lot of our eating "just happens" between engagements or projects. We may be in the mall passing time before a doctor's appointment. A good time to sit down with a cup of coffee and a sweet roll? No. We may have finished writing a letter and before we take the dog to the groomer, we stop to grab a snack. Somehow we don't remember these tasty tidbits—but our bodies do. We need to get in the habit of writing down *everything* we eat. We may be surprised not only at the amount but also at the quality of stuff we're stuffing.

It's no secret that fat can kill us. It's no secret that caffeine and sugar and empty calories will one day show up on our nerves, our teeth, and our hips. Determine with me today to make it a good habit to faithfully record what and how much of everything that goes into your mouth. Book 'im!

# Clue:

> To avoid a weight gain plight,
> I'll take the time to write,
> To plan my meals just right,
> And adopt the "food diary" rite.

# Diet Data:

Don't be disappointed if you aren't losing megapounds megafast! To lose a pound of fat, you need to burn up thirty-five hundred calories over what your body requires. See your doctor to learn what a reasonable calorie intake is for you. Slow and easy—remember?

# Solution:

Do not let this Book of the Law depart from your mouth; meditate on it day and night, so you may be careful to do everything written in it. Then you will be prosperous and successful.

Joshua 1:8

Have I established the habit of writing down my daily food intake?

Why is it important for me to keep track of what I eat?

Do I carefully measure my foods because I know my eyes can deceive me?

How much can one extra helping hurt?

Am I choosing foods I enjoy?

Why is it important, for my long-range goal, to eat not only nutritiously but also pleasurably?

Instead of writing down my menu *after* I eat, today I will plan
my food intake *before* the day begins.

Breakfast:

Lunch:

Dinner:

*Two* planned snacks:

# Breaking and Entering
## (Exercise)

## Evidence:

Well, I guess it's time for me to *break* out of my four walls and *enter* the world of exercise. I've never been the athletic type. In fact, every attempt at any sport has left me bruised, battered, or sitting on my backside. My beautiful ten-speed bike has more cobwebs than spokes because I can't gear up to gear down. My tennis racket has a broken handle. I tripped over it trying to perfect my backswing. Swimming? Sorry. Lessons with the city's best left my instructors holding their sides with laughter and me holding onto the edge of the pool.

I've tried bowling (three trips down the gutter were enough for me), volleyball (how many people have you ever seen who could hang themselves on the net), and golf. My club went farther than the ball down the fairway. I did pursue jogging for several years without falling over my own feet, but my knees eventually cried "uncle," so I stopped that, too.

What can I possibly do to get my heart rate up and my muscles toned? All the experts tell us that aerobic exercise on a regular basis not only helps us to lose weight but also to maintain the loss. Aerobic or cardiovascular exercise is sustained activity involving the large muscle groups, especially the legs. It increases the amount of oxygen processed by the body, making the lungs more efficient and a heart attack less likely. Not only will I have the benefit of losing weight, I'll also be physically fit. The way I see it, I need to find an activity that I enjoy. Otherwise I won't continue day after day.

After weighing the pros and cons (mostly cons), I decided that walking fills the bill. It doesn't cost me anything. I don't have to have a cute sweat suit or expensive running shoes. My doctor's last report was that my heart is healthy and walking can be only a benefit to me. I even have a friend who is willing to take me on as a partner every morning. Karen and I used to walk together regularly, and I look forward to again sharing that forty-five minutes with her.

If only I can keep from tripping over the cracks in the sidewalk!

## Hey, Partner:

What kind of exercise will you choose? If you're out of shape and haven't participated in any form of exercise for quite a while, please don't begin until you get the okay from your doctor. If you have any history of cardiovascular problems, or if you develop unexpected symptoms of dizziness or breathlessness, you need to let a physician recommend the type of exercise program that is best for you. Remember to be patient with yourself. It took years to grow into a nice, lumpy couch potato, so it will take time to peel away some of that excess poundage.

I started my exercise program with one-mile hikes, which took me twenty to twenty-five minutes. Now, after five months of walking three to four times a week, I've increased my mileage to three and decreased my time to fifteen minutes per mile. My body is beginning to yearn for more time on the path, so I'm going to increase my walking period to one hour a day.

I would like to mention that if you don't have a safe neighborhood to walk in, you can find walking partners in many of the malls. Mall-walking has become a popular way to exercise. Nurses and physical therapists are there to monitor your vitals and offer advice. You'll find as you exercise (whatever form you choose) that the psychological benefits are as beneficial as the physical ones. Aerobic exercise reduces anxiety and tension as well as thighs. It can decrease blood pressure and resting heart rate. God gave us bodies with muscles and tendons that need to be stretched, and hearts and lungs that need to be expanded. Let's give them back to Him—healthy and physically fit—by *breaking* away from our old sedentary life-style and *entering* the world of exercise!

## Clue:

> Weighted down with troubles,
> I've often run ahead,
> But I'm learning to slow down
> And walk with God instead.

## Diet Data:

Walking burns about one hundred calories per mile, so if you want to burn more, add an extra mile and a hill or two.

You can listen to your favorite "praise" tapes to pick up your speed and enthusiasm.

## Solution:

> Walk in all the way that the Lord your God has commanded you, so that you may live and prosper and prolong your days in the land that you will possess.
>
> Deuteronomy 5:33

Am I fit?

How often do I exercise?

How does regular exercise improve my health?

How will regular exercise facilitate my weight loss?

What type of exercise most fits my life-style? Why?

I will contact my doctor for his advice on my exercise program.

With my doctor's okay, I will begin to exercise at least fifteen minutes a day, three days a week.

I will not only keep track of my food intake each day but I also will record my exercise schedule.

Each month I will increase the time I spend in exercise until I am exercising at least an hour a day, four times a week.

How has God led me to walk in His way? *See* the Solution. Be specific.

# The Case of the Shattered Window

## (False Accusations)

## Evidence:

"Does your son have a BB gun?" The woman shot the words at me the instant I opened my front door.

"Well, yes, but it's a very old one and—"

She narrowed her eyes and spoke through clenched teeth. "He shot a hole through my bedroom window!"

"Are you sure it was my son?"

"Are you calling me a liar?"

I wasn't exactly calling her a liar, but I certainly couldn't imagine how my ten-year-old boy could shoot a hole through that neighbor's window. Her house was at least twenty feet beyond the six-foot-high fence that surrounded our backyard. And the gun was an old, weak thing that could propel a BB no farther than six feet. We had allowed him to have it for that very reason.

"There's no way my son could have damaged your window," I insisted. "The gun is old and—"

"You'll be getting a bill from me!" she blurted before turning on her heel. "And if you don't pay, I'll get the police."

Later that evening I questioned my son. Then we went outside and tested the gun.

*Pop*—and drop!

The BB went three feet into the air and fell to the ground.

I knew the neighbor's window had been shattered by someone else's gun. But whose?

Satisfied that my son was innocent, I went ahead and paid for her window in order to keep peace in the neighborhood. Two weeks later when I was in my backyard, I heard a popping sound. I peeked through the fence to see the same neighbor's college-age son aiming his BB pistol at a coffee can.

Case dismissed.

# Hey, Partner:

It is an unhappy feeling to have someone bring false charges against us. How good it is, though, when there is someone in our corner to defend us. My boy was upset when I suggested he might have broken the neighbor's window, but I assured him that I believed in his innocence and stood by him. When I paid the bill for the window, I reminded my neighbor that I knew my son hadn't broken it but that I chose to pay for it anyway.

Has anyone brought charges against you in your endeavor to lose weight? Sometimes a friend or family member will (unknowingly?) accuse us of being self-centered or thoughtless.

Example: "I baked this pie especially for you, and you're not going to eat any of it?"

"I never know what to fix for dinner now that you're on that stupid diet—again!"

"Aren't you getting too thin? You might get sick if you lose any more weight."

These are false charges. We are accused of taking care of ourselves. We are guilty of self-control.

What is our defense in the face of such accusations?

We have our food plan, which is well balanced and nutritious. We have a new alertness and spring to our step. We have a fresh sense of good health and a genuine concern for the health of our loved ones.

Case dismissed.

But these are not our only accusers. Satan, who is also called "the accuser of our brethren" (Revelation 12:10 KJV) continually shoots his darts at us. He taunts us when we're tired; he operates on us with his favorite tool, discouragement, when we feel weak; and he blasts us with accusations when we are happy.

"What right do you have to feel so good when there are millions of people dying of hunger every day?"

"What's the use of exercising self-control? It just makes you miserable."

"Why should you care if you are disciplined in your eating habits? You'll probably lose all your friends."

Satan uses other themes for his attacks, too. He tells us we are too sinful for God to love. He whispers that we should put ourselves under legalism if we expect God's blessings. And he suggests that after all is said and done, we will probably be lost anyway. What a liar.

Jesus said, ". . . [the devil] is a liar and the father of lies" (John 8:44).

Regardless of Satan's accusations, we have a Defender in our corner. Jesus Christ, we are told in 1 John 2:1, "speaks to the Father in our defense."

Case dismissed.

# Clue:

> Satan aims his BB gun
> Right between my eyes.
> But the devil can't hurt me
> If I don't believe his lies.

# Diet Data:

If your diet program is becoming a burdensome chore, try to evaluate why. Then consider the problems not as burdens but as challenges. Don't give up now. You've come this far one day at a time. Continue to live in the present. The past is irretrievable. The future is always out of reach. Today is yours.

# Solution:

> Now have come the salvation and the power and the
>    kingdom of our God,
>    and the authority of his Christ.
> For the accuser of our brothers,
>    who accuses them before our God day and night,
>    has been hurled down.
> They overcame him
>    by the blood of the Lamb
>    and by the word of their testimony. . . .
>                           Revelation 12:10, 11a

How do I handle false accusations regarding my weight loss?

In what way am I my own accuser?

Is it always necessary to defend myself against false accusations? Why? Why not?

95

What accusation does Satan use most on me?

How can I resist Satan's lies? Write out at least two Scripture verses to back my answer.

Why does Jesus have such great power over Satan?

# Things That Go Bump in the Night

## (Unfounded Fears)

## Evidence:

I usually sleep on my side now. How many potbellies do you know who can comfortably sleep on their tummies? Actually, I like sleeping on my side except for the problem of what to do with my arms. I don't know whether to tuck them under the pillow, in which case I awake with tingly hands that feel like boxing gloves, or wrap them around myself. Last week I evidently fell asleep on my left side with my left arm somehow draped across my front and my hand resting lightly on my right shoulder. Get the picture?

Something woke me out of a delightful dream about a huge

banquet table laden with cakes and cookies—oh, let's not dwell on that—and as I became conscious of my surroundings, I noticed a bump on the shoulder under my left hand. Carefully I circled the hard lump with my fingers, while my heart raced in fear. A tumor! I had a tumor on my shoulder. As I lay there in the dark, contemplating my future without an arm, my husband snored on, oblivious to my concern.

I slept very little the rest of the night because I found it a good time not only to worry about the possible amputation of my arm but also to allow countless other worries to traipse across the screen of my imagination. How would my children feel about a mother with only one arm? Would Les help me with the cooking? How would I drive? Or write?

I decided not to discuss my finding with Les until I had seen a doctor. When I told the nurse it was an emergency, I was given an appointment that very afternoon.

"Now, what's the problem?" The doctor saw the concern on my face.

"I've found a hard lump—and, well, I think it might be a tumor." I fought back the tears as once again a one-armed yet svelte figure danced across the stage of my mind.

His brows furrowed as he leaned toward me. "Where is this hard lump? How long has it been since you've had a mammogram?"

"Oh, no, doctor, it's here." I dropped the neckline of my paper gown and pointed at the bump on my shoulder.

"That's it?" His gloved fingers carefully traced the lump.

"Yes. I found it last night. Do you think it's malignant?"

"Have you looked at your other shoulder?" he asked, with a twinkle in his eye.

"Why, no. I didn't think to examine my left shoulder."

The twinkle erupted into a laugh. "Mrs. Cook, you've been

losing weight, and . . ." more laughter ". . . and that bump you're so worried about is only a bone. It's supposed to be there!"

I didn't know whether to join in the laughter or cry with relief, so instead I just mumbled an apology for taking his time and covered my red face with both hands.

## Hey, Partner:

What unfounded fears hold you in their grip? You may be aware of concerns over cancer or heart disease, but as the layers of fat begin to melt away, you might find yourself facing fears that have been long hidden behind the wall of excess weight. Some of us actually fear weight loss because we feel we're losing ourselves. That extra girth gave us a sense of strength and power.

As our bodies become smaller, our awareness of emotions, vulnerabilities, and pain may surface. But we don't have to be afraid, because those fears are not real. Our emotions are healthy and we can learn to enjoy them instead of drowning them with food. To be vulnerable is not a weakness but a strength. Who was more vulnerable than the Lord Jesus Christ? He felt not only His own pain but the pain and suffering of every man, woman, and child on earth.

Let's thank God for what He is doing in our hearts as we murder FAT. We're growing in character as our bodies shrink.

## Clue:

> What I believed was a tumor
> Was all in my head.
> What I thought was a tragedy
> Was a triumph instead.

## Diet Data:

Cooking in cast iron raises the iron content of food. Try simmering spaghetti sauce and soups for at least three hours for a healthy dose of iron.

## Solution:

There is no fear in love. But perfect love drives out fear, because fear has to do with punishment. . . .

1 John 4:18a

How many diets have I failed to complete?

Could I be afraid to reach my goal?

What fears do I have about being thin?

Look at each fear logically. Are these unfounded fears? Why?

The Solution states that "perfect love drives out fear." What does that statement mean to me?

Today by faith I let go of my unfounded fears to trust in God's love.

Signature_____Date_____

# The Inner Sanctum
## (Quiet Time)

### Evidence:

When I was a child, one of my family's favorite pastimes was to sit around the radio and listen to mysteries. Among our preferred programs was one which began with the sound of a squeaking door and an invitation into a half hour of mystery and intrigue: "The Inner Sanctum."

I always got the shivers when I heard that door creak. One Halloween, for extra scare appeal, I decided to add similar sound effects to our annual reception of goblins and ghosts. A recording of squeaking doors, howling wolves, and high-pitched screeches would add to the fun of passing out candy bars and chocolate kisses. (I only give out what I love. After all, there might be some leftovers.)

That afternoon, one of my daughters and her little friend were in the living room planning their costumes and listening to the record. I was in the kitchen sampling the treats when I heard a squeal. "Boy, your mom sure made it look scary in here."

"Oooh, wow!" exclaimed my daughter. Then, "Mom where did you get such a real-looking spiderweb? It's so spooky!"

Spooky? I hadn't decorated the living room. I jammed the last bite of a candy bar into my mouth and went to see what the excitement was all about. My eyes followed the pointing fingers of two little girls to a wispy mass draped from the ceiling to a lampshade A real-life Halloween spiderweb stretched across the corner of the seldom-used room, all the more visible because the lamp had been turned on.

"Oh, Mrs. Cook," added the little girl in a witch's hat, "your cheeks are so round and rosy. I bet you're gonna be a clown for Halloween, huh?"

"No, schweetie," I hissed, dropping a piece of last year's bubble gum into her bag before escorting her to the door. "Clowns laugh. I'm not laughing right now."

Who says honesty in children is an adorable trait?

My lack of housekeeping abilities in the inner sanctum of my home had come to light. Not until that lamp had been turned on was the cobweb, and my embarrassment, revealed. After devouring a few more candy kisses, I felt brave enough to turn on more lights, get out the feather duster, and go to work.

## Hey, Partner:

Just as that light exposed cobwebs in my living room corner, the light of God's Word shines on sins, such as laziness and gluttony, that have crept into my life. And I need that. In fact, the longer I continue in this weight-management plan, the more I see my need to rely upon God and His living Word.

Without a daily quiet time spent reading the Bible and communing with the Lord, I neglect to turn on the light in my inner sanctum. And that neglect fosters growth of sin in the darkened corners of my heart.

When I began this weight-loss program, I found that the excitement of melting pounds kept me going. But as the months pass, so does the drive to continue my newly learned skills. And when I think ahead to the days and years before me, I feel apprehensive. Will I be able to reach my ideal weight—then maintain the loss?

No, not by myself. Not even the encouragement of a diet group can take me over the hurdles of the future. I (and you, partner) need something, Someone, whose power is greater than our own. And that Someone has made a promise that is renewable daily as we meet with Him in the inner sanctum, the holy place: "Never will I leave you; never will I forsake you" (Hebrews 13:5).

As we grow more reliant upon God instead of food, we will become more open to His guidance and light. We will confess our sins and be made clean. We will begin to walk in His will instead of our own. We will find that our old habits and routines are being replaced by new creative thoughts and actions.

Let's not neglect the most important aspect of our weight management: daily communication with the Lord of glory!

## Clue:

A cobweb in the corner
Is not a pretty sight.
If I don't want to see it,
I won't turn on the light.

## Diet Data:

Believe it or not, skipping meals will slow down the weight-loss process. You can actually burn between one hundred and two hundred calories by eating three meals a day. Even more calories can be consumed by chewing crunchy foods such as celery and carrot sticks.

## Solution:

O God, you are my God,
    earnestly I seek you;
my soul thirsts for you,
    my body longs for you,
in a dry and weary land
    where there is no water.
I have seen you in the sanctuary
    and beheld your power and your glory.
Because your love is better than life,
    my lips will glorify you.
I will praise you as long as I live,
    and in your name I will lift up my hands.
My soul will be satisfied as with the richest of foods;
    with singing lips my mouth will praise you.

Psalm 63:1–5

Why is it important to my continued weight loss to spend time alone meditating upon God and His Word?

Why is God's Word referred to as "light"?

What sins or lack of obedience does today's Solution expose in my life?

Why is it futile to attempt to control my eating habits by sheer willpower?

To the overeater, surrender to God is the only way to continued victory. Do I believe this? Why? Why not?

Compare how God satisfies my soul with the way rich foods satisfy my appetite.

# Corpus Delicti
## (Body Image)

### Evidence:

I stepped out of the shower and stood before the full-length mirror. That was a middle-aged mirror if I ever saw one! Its chin drooped. In fact, everything from the chin down to the ankles drooped. And what didn't droop, bulged! My corpus delicti was material evidence that a crime had taken place. I pinched a couple of inches, wishing I could pinch them right off and toss them into the wastebasket. *Ouch!*

I had lost about eight pounds, but I still looked fat. I had about two-thirds more to go. Could I make it? I continued to survey my body from head to toe. How did I feel about it? Did I hate my own body? Or did I love it? Well, there were some parts I could tolerate, but all in all it was definitely a love/hate relationship. I hated my fat stomach, yet I was thankful that I didn't have to eat or eliminate through tubes. I hated my cellulited thighs, but I was glad my legs were not paralyzed or amputated. I had both breasts, both arms, and both chins. My body was healthy in spite of my mistreatment of it.

I looked again, this time with appreciation and gratitude to the Lord God for His ingenious creativity. After several months, I would have the body He originally had designed for me. The pads of fat would be gone, the muscles toned, and there would be a smile instead of a frown on my face. I had begun a good work with God's guidance and strength, and with Him I would complete it. This corpus delicti would soon be a corpus delicious!

# Hey, Partner:

Have you taken a good long look at your body lately, or does your mirror reflect only your neck and face? Try to observe every part of your body without anger and judgment. True, you may have disfigured it with food; you may have parts that are scarred or even missing. But just see yourself as you are and say aloud, "I love my body!" For until we learn to love this remarkable gift God has given us, we won't care for it properly.

Do you throw your best piece of jewelry on the floor? Do you dust the furniture with that expensive silk blouse? No. You take good care of those things you consider valuable. And you cherish the gifts given to you by those who love you.

My husband may not give me diamonds, but when he does present me with a gift, I love it because it is an expression of his love. How do you feel about the Giver of Life? He loves you and me. Our opinions of our bodies as well as our response to God will determine how we treat or mistreat the most precious of God's gifts: our lives encased in flesh-and-blood bodies.

You may not like the shape of your nose or the color of your skin, but each and every part of you was designed by God and is best suited for your own personal use: to honor and glorify Him.

". . . Shall what is formed say to him who formed it, 'Why did you make me like this?' " (Romans 9:20b).

As we begin by faith to thank God for our bodies, just as they are today, we will be released from the anger we've been unleashing on ourselves. Make friends with that body of yours—it's been with you for a long time, and if you continue to take good care of it, it will be with you even longer.

## Clue:

> Mirror, mirror on the wall,
> Am I too short or too tall?
> Did God make a mistake in creating me?
> Can I love and accept what I see?

## Diet Data:

Did you know that drinking tea or coffee with your meal can reduce your iron absorption by nearly 50 percent? If you start a meal with orange or tomato juice, you can double the amount of iron absorbed from the iron-rich food in your diet.

## Solution:

> Now we see but a poor reflection . . . then we shall see face to face. Now I know in part; then I shall know fully, even as I am fully known. And now these three remain: faith, hope and love. But the greatest of these is love.
>                                        1 Corinthians 13:12, 13

Corpus Delicti (Body Image)

Today I will look at my nude body in a full-length mirror.

Does my mental image match my physical image? How? How not?

Do I base my self-image on negative feelings from my childhood? Recall and write down those feelings.

Do I think I should be and look perfect? Why?

Does God's Word state that God loves us because of our looks or actions? "This is love: not that we loved God, but that he loved us and sent his Son as an atoning sacrifice for our sins" (1 John 4:10).

How does God show His love to us?

Romans 13:9 tells us to love ourselves: "Love your neighbor as yourself." By faith, I will love myself as God loves me—including all my imperfections. I will say aloud, "God loves me as I am—and I love myself—my body, my emotions, my life, and all that entails, and I thank God for this gift of life!"

I will now write five times: "I love my body and all God has given to me."

# You Have the Right to Right to Remain Silent
## (Choices)

## Evidence:

"Well, I've tried every diet there is, and I still can't lose weight. I've decided that all these diets and preoccupation with nutrition and overweight is some kind of Communist plot!"

Miranda's voice droned on and on in the back of my mind. It seemed she had been discussing her weight problem for years. In fact, I'd known her for three years and knew little else about her. She was always "on" or "off" her diet. I focused my eyes on her as she spoke about her new freedom. "I'm happier now than I've ever been," she said, digging into a heaping bowl of fudge-covered ice cream.

Miranda's weight had won the battle. She had put on ten more pounds since I last saw her. And she wasn't happy, in spite of her forced smile. I knew, because I had said the same words only a few months before.

I've found that the more I discuss my problem of over-weight (or any other problem, for that matter), the more control it seems to exert over me. And besides, my struggles with overweight are of little interest to anyone else. How many times have I seen my husband's eyes glaze over while I moped, "I feel so fat. I wish I could lose some weight. I don't have anything to wear. I wish I could have a candy bar instead of this apple. I. . .I. . .I. . . ."

*Bo-ring!*

I mentioned earlier in the chapter "Murder on the FAT Express'" the importance of confessing my food addiction to a trusted friend, but that doesn't mean I should continually bend every ear that leans my way. If I quit talking about diets and do something about my problem, not only will I stop irritating my friends and family, I'll also gain new strength in overcoming both problems: overeating and overtalking.

Do my overweight friends want a guilt trip as I point out to them what they should or should not eat? Do my thin friends care one way or the other how many calories I ate for break-fast? I may find that by the time I've lost weight, I've also lost some friends along the way.

You have the right to remain silent—about your gains and losses, and about your successes and failures.

As Miranda and I left the restaurant, she sighed and turned to me. "That was a great sundae, but I wish I hadn't eaten it." A tear glistened in the corner of her eye.

# Hey, Partner:

Sometimes we wear ourselves and others out by the con-tinual discussion of our problems. It's true that we do need and cherish our friends and want to be open with them. But we ought to ask ourselves, *Am I being selfish in this relationship? Am I draining my friend by constantly unloading my burdens on her?*

We do have choices—rights. God has given us many: when to speak and when to remain silent; we can continue to over-eat and complain that we are fat, or we can take control of what goes into and what comes out of our mouths. We do not have to make friends; we can isolate ourselves and find consolation from food. We do not have to learn weight management—and we do not have to overeat. But best of all, we do not have to bear any of the burdens of life alone; we can commit our lives, with all the ups and downs, to our Lord. Jesus Christ knows and understands every problem, every worry, every anxious thought you and I suffer—and He can give us His power to overcome those weighty issues that keep us running off at the mouth.

Yes, we have the right to remain silent, the right to speak, the right to overeat, the right to control our eating. We also have the right to turn our lives over to God, or we can continue to bear the burden of our own selfishness and misery. What's it going to be?

## Clue:

> A donut or an apple,
> Which shall it be?
> A complaint or a prayer,
> The decision falls on me.

## Diet Data:

Giving in to an urge for chocolate doesn't really satisfy. It only enforces and strengthens the craving. Choose to let the urge pass, and you'll find its control over you has weakened.

Instead of giving in to those cravings, plan to treat yourself, say on Saturday night, with *one* or *two* bites of chocolate. You won't sabotage your diet or your self-esteem.

## Solution:

. . . Now choose life, so that you and your children may live and that you may love the Lord your God, listen to his voice, and hold fast to him. For the Lord is your life, and he will give you many years in the land he swore to give to your fathers, Abraham, Isaac and Jacob.

Deuteronomy 30:19b, 20

Do I find my preoccupation with dieting the primary source of my conversations?

Am I a good listener?

Does talking about my weight problem help or hinder my progress? How?

What positive action other than talking will help me lose weight?

List three subjects other than diet/weight that interest me.
1.
2.
3.

Today I will handle my cravings by:

# You're Under Arrest!
## (Binges)

## Evidence:

What a day! I cleaned house, washed the car, did the grocery shopping, and even managed to fix a nutritious, well-balanced dinner. Then my youngest daughter called to say she had been in an accident. She was okay, but the car was banged up and would be in the shop for six weeks. She had no way to get to school. She hung up in tears, and I hung up totally frustrated. What could I do to help? She attended college four hundred miles away, and—the phone rang again. It was the oldest daughter. Her application to teach English in China had been accepted. She would be moving out of her apartment and making arrangements to spend a year in a Communist country.

After Les and I discussed these news bulletins, he went off to bed and I sat on the couch alone. I was too keyed up to sleep, and I didn't want to think about Barby's accident or

Kathy's future, so I switched on the TV to escape my own weariness and worries.

Memories of the day disappeared as James Rockford pursued a rerun mystery assignment. I was hungry. What would fit into my food plan and still satisfy the urges pulling at my emotions? An apple? *Yuck.* Some celery with salsa? *Gag.* Low-cal hot chocolate? *Give me a break.* I rummaged through the cupboard. Why didn't I have any goodies stashed away for such an emergency? The more I looked, the hungrier I became. I found some stale rice cakes and slightly stiff peanut butter. One or two would satisfy me for sure.

They didn't taste good enough, so during the next commercial I went on another treasure hunt. On the bottom shelf of the buffet, I found a half bag of peanut M&M's left over from Easter, and in the back of the freezer was a chunk of Christmas fruitcake. Down they went. Still not satisfied but beginning to feel miserable, I went on one last hunt. Something salty would take away that icky sweet taste: a few crackers and a glass of orange juice.

Rockford finally got his man, and I finally felt sick enough to stop eating.

"You're under arrest!" came the voice from the corner of the room. The runaway criminal had been brought to justice; the credits ran across the screen; and another commercial flashed on. I sat there feeling miserable. I was still tired from the day's work, Barby was still four hundred miles away with no transportation to school, and Kathy was still making plans to fly off into no-man's-land. Les was peacefully sleeping in the back of the house, and I was sick. Sick of myself. My appetite had taken control of me after that first unplanned bite of food, and instead of taking me out of my worries, the binge had given me another anxiety.

"You're under arrest!" I heard myself say aloud. "Binging does not and will never satisfy my craving." My food addiction is like a criminal. I must arrest it and keep it under lock and key, or it will kill me not only emotionally and spiritually but eventually physically as well.

That night before falling into bed, I knelt down to confess my sin to the Lord. Why hadn't I taken my anxieties to Him instead of looking to fiction and food to relieve them? He alone is able to truly satisfy.

## Hey, Partner:

Let's get a search warrant and seriously begin to investigate our personal eating disorders. We may be able to follow a food regimen for weeks or even months, then one day (or night) something sets us off on a binge. We may think that after we get our weight under control we can then eat spontaneously. The problem with that kind of thinking is that food never completely satisfies. Contentment is not found through the taste buds. We imagine that there was a time when food made us feel happy, and we try to recapture that euphoric sensation. But the more we eat, the more we want to eat—and the worse we feel. When we discover the answer to true contentment and conscientiously follow our food plan, we will finally bring our out-of-control appetites under arrest.

## Clue:

When I was tired and worried,
I turned to cookies and cake.
But instead of peace and comfort,
I got a stomachache.

## Diet Data:

Try adding two tablespoons of powdered diet gelatin and one teaspoon of diet preserves to plain nonfat yogurt for a yummy low-calorie dessert. Keep on hand for those late-night hungries.

## Solution:

You open your hand
    and satisfy the desires of every living thing.
                                                    Psalm 145:16

Recall the last time I binged on food. What set if off?

You're Under Arrest! (Binges)

Where was I and what did I eat?

How did I feel during the binge?

How did I feel after the binge?

Can I honestly say that food gives me genuine comfort?

List some alternatives to binging?

Read the Solution again. What does this verse mean to me?

# Preliminary Hearing
## (Forgiveness)

## Evidence:

I woke up with a hangover—literally. Not only my stomach but also my eyelids were bloated. My hands had ten plump wieners hanging off them, and I was depressed. Why, oh, why had I done it to myself? Why had I sat up alone to stuff my face? *I'm awful! I'm a failure. I can't stay on a diet. I'm not always a cheerful wife or a patient mother. I haven't written to my best friend in months, and I forgot my cousin's birthday. What kind of person am I?*

"You are a human being," I heard a voice from deep within say. "You will never be perfect and until you accept that fact, you will continue to flagellate yourself for setbacks and slip-ups."

The voice, wherever it came from, was right. I thought back to the many times I had allowed depression to control my life when I had failed to perform to my own expectations.

So I had overeaten last night. I was paying for it already this morning. I didn't need to bring up every goof I had made in the past.

When I looked at myself in the bathroom mirror, I forced a smile and lifted my chin (no, not chins. My weight loss was showing on my face and body). I had confessed my sin of gluttony and instant gratification last night. Now all I needed was to forgive myself. I deserved a preliminary hearing—not a conviction.

I remembered a statement by Corrie ten Boom that went something like this: "When we confess our sin, God buries it in the deepest sea, then puts up a sign that says, 'No Fishing.' " If God could forgive my sins, why was it so difficult for me to let go of them?

Perfectionism.

Ego.

Self.

That preliminary hearing uncovered evidence that, in spite of my weaknesses, God loves and accepts me as I am. Not only that, He gives me the power and courage to accept myself along with my setbacks and failures. I am not perfect and never will be, but I am progressing even as I learn from my mistakes and self-will.

## Hey, Partner:

Are you human? If so, your determination never to slip up in your weight-loss program may weaken now and then. Your lapse of memory in keeping a food diary or an occasional fall into a binge could make you feel, "I might as well give up" or "I'm a failure anyway." And that kind of guilt trip can convict you before the jury comes in. Give yourself a fair hearing. You need a friend in your corner—and that friend is *you*. Would you be as hard on one of your family members or dearest friends if any of them came to you for encouragement? No, you would listen patiently, offer words of support and hope, and send your friend on his way. Do the same for yourself.

Your defense attorney, Jesus Christ, knows all about you. He has prepared evidence in your favor, and He has taken any punishment you deserve. So be good to yourself as you pursue this long process of weight loss. You know you can stay on the plan for one day at a time because you've done it before. You can forgive yourself for not measuring up to your own out-of-reach standards, put yesterday behind you, pick up your determination, and continue the journey to health and fitness. After all, this is a lifetime change—not a diet to go "on" and "off." You can cut through the red tape, refuse to be a victim, and walk away free—released from the bondage of perfectionism!

## Clue:

A little Goody-Two-Shoes—
That's what I tried to be,
Till I tripped on a broken shoestring,
And fell and skinned my knee.

## Diet Data:

Something red, something green, something hot, something cold, something smooth, something crunchy. Try to eat a variety of foods at each meal, not only for good nutrition but also for satisfaction. Include foods from different groups; also try different colors and textures. A meal should satisfy your eyes, your taste buds, and your physical requirements.

# Solution:

When you were dead in your sins and in the uncircum-cision of your sinful nature, God made you alive with Christ. He forgave us all our sins, having canceled the written code, with its regulations, that was against us and that stood opposed to us; he took it away, nailing it to the cross. And having disarmed the powers and authorities, he made a public spectacle of them, triumphing over them by the cross.

Colossians 2:13–15

Is there anyone in my life I need to forgive?

Could my overweight be connected to my reluctance to forgive?

Am I harboring unforgiveness toward myself? Why?

Write the words in the Solution that tell of God's forgiveness.

How do I display perfectionism?

How will giving up my perfectionism release me to serve others?

# Do You Have an Alibi?
## (Holidays)

## Evidence:

I scanned the pages of the calendar. Next week was Greg's birthday, then his and Carol's anniversary. I couldn't hurt their feelings by not eating some of their cakes. Could I? Two weeks later, it would be Barby's birthday, then Thanksgiving, then Mother's and Christy's birthdays—then Christmas. Oh, how would I ever get through the holidays without adding my usual ten pounds?

I had been following the food plan faithfully (somewhat) for months now and had lost enough weight to begin feeling pretty terrific. Could I set aside all I had learned for the next two months of celebrations and the special food and desserts that would be available?

I needed to solve the mystery of Christmas past and bring my false alibis into custody.

I thought back to other years. There was always some event

that involved a big dinner topped by an elegant dessert. Between those times of feasting were "Candyland" specials such as Valentine's Day and Halloween. I could always come up with an alibi: "As soon as Kathy's birthday is over, I'll go on a diet."

"After we come back from our vacation, I'll go on a diet."

After Christmas—after New Year's—after any possible reason to put off weight control.

Of course, with a family of six adult children which grows annually to include husbands, wives, and babies, our lives have become one continuous party. So far, since beginning this latest—and last—weight-loss plan, I've handled those events pretty well. But I can't let down now. I have to plan my strategy not only to enjoy the social atmosphere of the coming holiday season but also to avoid the obstacles so temptingly arranged on the buffet table. Wow, this puzzle of how to murder FAT is one that keeps me on my toes.

## Hey, Partner:

Whether you are counting calories or following some other plan of attack, you can enjoy whatever festivity is coming up next on your calendar. It only takes some investigative skills.

For instance, I've discovered it is not smart to arrive at a party hungry. We usually reason this way: "I won't eat any breakfast or lunch; then I can really enjoy [pig-out on] the dinner and all the desserts." But as a rule, when we arrive so hungry, we eat more than we would have if we had eaten two lighter meals during the day. Besides, it doesn't make a great impression on the hostess when we snatch the cheesecake off the plate next to us, then hurriedly devour not only the dessert but also the doily under it.

One way I've avoided the vacuum cleaner mentality is to decide what I'm going to eat before I arrive at a party. If there is a smorgasbord table, I'll choose vegetables and breadsticks, a few pieces of fruit, and maybe a small portion of meat. Then I get as far away from the table as possible, eat slowly, and enjoy the festivities and conversation.

I've watched the naturally thin partygoers and tried to imitate them. Do you know they don't eat everything on their plates? I've even seen thin people with dishes of melted ice cream. Can you believe it?

Another way to keep from feeling deprived is to take a small plate. It fills up quickly, and just the sight of a full plate seems to satisfy.

Tricks instead of treats.

So if your calendar is brimming with social engagements, birthday parties, and celebrations, don't let rigor mortis set in—get moving before the fact and use your powers of detection. We can be released from our bondage to the buffet. We can murder FAT and get away with it!

# Clue:

> I'm going to a party,
> And know I will have fun.
> Because I'm under God's control,
> I can eat just one.

# Diet Data:

When confronting a buffet loaded down with all kinds of sandwich fillings, keep your calorie count low by building your sandwich on lettuce leaves instead of bread. Choose the celery and carrot sticks to replace potato chips. And nothing satisfies thirst more than a glass of cold water. For dessert, a chunk of watermelon leaves a sweeter taste in the mouth than a chunk of chocolate cake. Besides, why wear a band of fat around your middle when you can show off a trimmer waistline with a wide belt?

## Solution:

All the days of the oppressed are wretched,
but a cheerful heart has a continual feast.

Proverbs 15:15

What's my favorite alibi (excuse) for deviating from my food plan?


Does the thought of "party eating" scare me? Why? Why not?


Write an M.O. (method of operation) for an upcoming celebration.


I believe I can face a buffet table with confidence because:


What does this Solution mean: "All the days of the oppressed are wretched. . . ."


What does "but a cheerful heart has a continual feast" mean to me?

# Circumstantial Evidence
## (Discoveries)

## Evidence:

I always enjoy driving to the Bay Area to spend a day and night with Becky and Dave and the grandchildren. I was especially pleased when she greeted me at the door with, "Mom, you've lost so much weight! You look great. I can even see your collarbones."

I told her how dedicated I was to losing the weight once and for all, and how I had learned new eating skills. I didn't keep such things as corn chips or peanut butter in the house anymore, and I felt in control of my obese mind-set. ("If you think you are standing firm, be careful you don't fall!")

It was a relaxing visit, as usual. The next afternoon after kissing the babies good-bye, I noticed I was missing one of my sculptured nails.

"Oh, Becky, I must have knocked a nail off when I took

out the garbage, or maybe when I was playing in Nicholas's room."

We searched the bedrooms and the bathroom and traced my steps to the car. No sign of that mauvey-pink plastic that gave my hands a longer, leaner look.

"Well, I suppose it's in the garbage can," I said, shutting the car door. "This is embarrassing. I hope Hannah doesn't find it while she's crawling through the kitchen."

"Don't worry," Becky assured me. "I'll run the vacuum right away. If it's on the floor, I'll get it."

I drove the hour and a half back home without another thought of the nail except replacing it as soon as possible.

Two days later, Becky called, "Mom, Dave found your fingernail."

*Oh, no.* "Where?"

"Well, I couldn't believe it when he told me—after what you said and all."

*Oh, dear.* I wasn't sure I wanted to hear the rest. "Where was it?" I said at last.

"In the peanut butter."

Silence.

"Mom?"

"Oh, Becky, I'm so embarrassed. How gross for Dave to find it at all—but in the peanut butter?"

"I didn't believe him at first," she said. "You told me you don't eat peanut butter anymore."

There was no getting out of this one. The circumstantial evidence had convicted me. I had sneaked into Becky's kitchen before going to sleep, and when I indulged in one of my favorite trigger foods, I left not a fingerprint but a fingernail.

I wonder how Dave feels about peanut butter after that grisly discovery. I wonder how he feels about me.

## Hey, Partner:

This is a gruesome but true story that brought me to a place where I was willing to make some discoveries about myself. It is difficult enough when someone else finds us out, but when we have to face our own shortcomings and sins, we may have to eat pie—humble pie.

I've discovered through these past months that while I'm learning to conquer my compulsive eating, I occasionally fall into compulsive spending. When I curb that desire, I compulsively clean or read. And, of course, there's always that compulsion to overtalk, which invariably releases pride. I don't particularly exult in this kind of discovery, but in addressing the dark, hidden side of my nature, I can find forgiveness and cleansing.

How can we dig up enough circumstantial evidence to make solid discoveries about ourselves? I don't mean we should always be digging up seeds to see if there is growth, but we do need to be tuned into God's still, small voice. He doesn't shout when we creep through the kitchen to poke a finger in the peanut butter, and He doesn't call our names when we dash out to our favorite department stores.

His voice is soft and barely audible. Only as we seek His guidance, by spending time in the Word of God and bowing before Him in prayer, will we be open to His leading. Genuine healing from obsessive behavior is possible. With God all things are possible.

What a discovery!

# Clue:

I like my acrylic nails,
But it makes me shudder
To think I lost one
In the peanut butter!

# Diet Data:

Drain three cups of nonfat plain yogurt in a cheesecloth-lined colander in the refrigerator overnight. Voilà! Cheese that measures only fifteen calories per tablespoon.

# Solution:

For there is nothing hidden that will not be disclosed,
and nothing concealed that will not be known or brought
out into the open.

Luke 8:17

Is there an area of my life that needs healing?

If I'm obsessive about eating, it is likely to overlap into other acts of compulsive behavior. List some possibilities in my life, such as spending, laziness, gossip.

Would I be willing to have all my secrets disclosed and brought out into the open?

Until I am willing to make discoveries of my hidden nature, I will not reach my full potential as a child of God. Write down some of those activities and/or thoughts that I keep buried.

Confess each and every activity or thought to God and accept His cleansing: "If we confess our sins, he is faithful and just and will forgive us our sins and purify us from all unrighteousness" (1 John 1:9).

# Person or Persons Unknown
## (Support)

## Evidence:

"I didn't want to come to the meeting today. I knew I had gained weight and dreaded facing the scale."

"I felt the same way," another woman groaned. "I just couldn't get control of my eating this week. I felt like a failure."

The woman next to me spoke up. "I know what you're saying, Debbie and Joan." (How did this cheerful, friendly woman remember the names of the other diet-group members?)

She went on, "I ate and ate this week, and although I've already lost fifteen pounds, I felt I hadn't accomplished anything these past months."

The bright-eyed lecturer spoke up. "But you are here—all of you. And aren't you glad you came?"

The woman next to me raised her hand. (Oh, why couldn't I recall her name? She always remembered mine. Let's see, it was something like Cashew or Pecan.)

The lecturer nodded in her direction. "Yes, Hazel?"

*Oh, now I get the connection.*

Hazel's smile was infectious. "I know I'm glad because I needed this encouragement. I need the rest of you," she said waving an arm over the group.

"Me, too," came a voice from the back of the room.

We all seemed to be nodding our heads up and down. We were in this together. We all had the same struggles, the same goals. We needed one another.

I glanced around the room again. This group, which seemed to grow week by week (in numbers, not girth), was my support group. Although I didn't know them by name, they were not persons unknown. They had allowed themselves to be vulnerable and genuine, and because of that we each had benefited. We were learning why we had become fat and how, once there, we could remain thin.

Let's hear it for the "person or persons unknown" in the diet group.

*Hip—hip—hooray! Hip—hip—hooray! Hip—hip—hooray!*

# Hey, Partner:

I can't begin to express how much that diet support group has meant to me. When I've been down, they lifted me up. When I wanted to give up and spend my vacation in Winchell's Donut Shop, they pulled me out of that hole. What lucky folks we are to have so many support groups to lean on. There are groups for almost any problem we might face: alcoholism and drug addiction; divorce; victims of violent crimes; abused wives and husbands; and the list goes on and on. We may think that support groups are something new, but the church, the pattern for many support groups, has been around for centuries.

Perhaps we think we don't need the church: "I can worship just as well in my own home, and I can study the Bible by myself better than with a group of people I don't know."

But just as I benefit from those who struggle with a similar weight problem, so there are those in the church who share like problems: loneliness, despair, frustration. We may feel shy about revealing our weaknesses with people we don't know, but as in my diet group, I've found people in the church who are not only willing but also eager to encourage me.

It is true that we can worship in our own homes where we may bow, weep, sigh, or shout (however the Spirit moves us). But you know, there's something about corporate worship in the body of Christ that enriches and inspires. Lifting our voices with a group of believers gives us not only a sense of belonging but also new strength in what can sometimes be a lonely walk along the path of life.

I can study the Bible on my own, too. As a Christian, I have the indwelling Holy Spirit to guide and teach me in the Word of God. However, through the combined insights of fellow believers, I can gain even more from my Bible study, and these people cease to be persons unknown.

I not only need a group to help me in my weight-loss endeavor but I also need the church to help me along my journey through the months and years ahead.

And believe it or not, the church (the people who make up each local congregation) needs me. It needs you. Because the church is Christ's body, every believer needs and is needed by the others.

When we stay away and look at the church from a distance, the men and women are persons unknown. Let's join this spiritual support group to worship God and study His Word together. Three cheers for the church!

*Hip—hip—hooray! Hip—hip—hooray! Hip—hip—hooray!*

# Clue:

Whether I'm weak and tired,
Whether I'm brave and strong,
I need you, and you need me
To help each other along.

# Diet Data:

Don't be discouraged if you've reached a weight plateau. Continue your weight-loss program, increase your exercise, and call a friend. If you belong to a diet group, go to a meeting for support. In time, your body will be ready to release more pounds.

# Solution:

And let us consider how we may spur one another on toward love and good deeds. Let us not give up meeting together, as some are in the habit of doing, but let us encourage one another—and all the more as you see the Day approaching.

Hebrews 10:24, 25

Am I a loner? Why? Why not?

When I have a problem, do I seek the help of a friend? Who?

Are there those who seek my help and advice? Who?

List the ways in which I encourage others.

How can a support group help me work my way through a problem?

If I am a Christian, how does the Solution apply to me?

# Keep a Lid on It!

## (Leftovers)

## Evidence:

What to do with that last half cup of spaghetti sauce. Not enough for another meal. Too much to throw away. So-o-o, I break off a chunk of French bread, swish it around in the pot, and toss it into the garbage can.

The one under the kitchen sink? No, the one attached to my neck! Before I even realized what I was doing, my round, unprotesting self was receiving the leftover scrapings of what had been a delicious meal.

Not only did I finish off the spaghetti sauce but in went the garlic bread and the rest of the green salad as well. I didn't really taste any of it. In fact, I don't think I was even aware of what I was doing. I simply reverted to old habits I had picked up when my children were small. In those days, I used to empty not only the pots and pans into my open mouth but I also managed to clean up the children's leftovers. Was it any wonder I had taken on the shape of a garbage can?

I had learned to be so frugal from my own childhood. My mother was insistent that I clean my plate before leaving the table. I often sat there for an hour after everyone else had left, still choking down lima beans. After all, those were depression years and food was a precious commodity.

Les and I weren't so demanding that our children clean their plates. The newer child-rearing books encouraged more freedom of choice. Our children served themselves and usually managed to eat what they had taken. But on those occasions when their judgment had failed, we let them be excused from the table without finishing their meals.

That's when my old training went into action. "Clean your plate. Waste not, want not. Think of all those starving children in China." Into the human "Waste Queen" went the leftovers.

That same bad habit lingered on into the present. There were no small children to clean up after now. Les and I were alone in the house. I had simply made too much sauce, and for several minutes I forgot my new food-management plan.

"What are you doing?" Les stopped on his way through the kitchen, either appalled or disgusted. I couldn't quite read his expression.

"Uh, I didn't want this stuff to go to waste."

"It will anyway," he said, shaking his head. "It'll go to your waist." He put his arms around me and squeezed. "And I like your waist the way it is now. You're really slimming down, honey. Don't do this to yourself." His soft brown eyes glistened.

That night I determined not to treat myself like a garbage can again. I'm keeping the lid on!

## Hey, Partner:

Have you ever had a garbage-can mentality? Are you still as troubled as I am by the thought of wasted food?

We need to relearn not only our eating habits but also our cooking habits. If for many years we cooked for a large family, we may find it difficult to prepare smaller portions today. We need to learn how to estimate how much food the remaining family members will consume at a meal.

I wonder if we sometimes prepare more than is necessary so we'll have an excuse to eat more.

Some cooks deliberately fix enough food for at least another meal. That can be a real time-saver if you've spent eight hours on the job and barely have time to pick the kids up at pre-school before dashing home for dinner. However, in order to keep from picking at next Tuesday's lasagna this Wednesday, wrap it well and stash it in the freezer.

How about leftover food that is difficult to estimate, such as a roast, a whole chicken, or even vegetables? We don't have to eat those tasty tidbits, nor do we have to throw away usable food. One lady I know puts all her leftovers into a freezer bowl for several weeks. Then on a cold blustery night, she serves a delicious soup made up of those little bits of meat and vegetables. Instead of smidgens of leftover yummies getting us into trouble, they can become nourishing stuff—just like Grandma used to make.

Let's decide, partner, to keep the lid on our own personal garbage can by lifting the lid of the freezer bowl and tossing those leftovers into it.

Our bodies are temples, not trash cans!

# Clue:

I'm shaped like a cylinder,
So let's face it, man:
I've turned my body
Into a garbage can!

# Diet Data:

Think thin by putting a picture on your refrigerator of the slender person you'd like to be. After a day or two, post it on your bathroom mirror, then on your closet door. This image will begin to impress you with the possibility of your new self. You are not a garbage can.

# Solution:

Do you not know that your body is a temple of the Holy Spirit, who is in you, whom you have received from God? You are not your own; you were bought at a price. Therefore honor God with your body.

1 Corinthians 6:19, 20

Is it difficult for me to leave food on my plate?

Do I feel I need to dispose of the food on the family's plates by eating it? What is my usual response to uneaten food?

Why is it hard for me to throw leftover food away?

Do I have an inner fear of hunger? Of famine conditions? Why?

What is meant by the statement, "Your body is a temple of the Holy Spirit" (1 Corinthians 6:19)?

How should that statement affect my eating habits?

# "I" Did It!
## (Pride)

## Evidence:

What could be more invigorating than early morning in the mountains? Not only was I in one of my favorite places, I was also with a group of Christian women at a weekend retreat. But what excited me most of all was that "I" was to lead that Saturday-morning group in a diet seminar. *Me!*

I had the work sheets all photocopied and my session well planned and laid out. I dressed in what I thought was a slimming outfit and bustled into the room full of enthusiasm. Boy, oh boy, did I have some good things to tell them.

"I" did this . . .

"I" did that . . .

"I" ate this . . .

"I" ate that . . .

The hour-long meeting seemed to go well and "I" felt pretty proud of my presentation. But something was amiss. As we mingled and talked before the next gathering, I felt that the women were looking at me funny. When I caught their eyes, they quickly turned away and (Was that a snicker I heard?) began to talk with one another. I could understand their not rushing over to include me in their conversations because I was an outsider from another city, but what was it about me that brought smiles to their faces?

I decided not to be concerned and jammed my hands into the pockets of my denim skirt. A rush of cold air caused me to look down. I had forgotten to fasten the hooks and eyes on the front of my skirt. I had massive gaposis!

Quickly I excused myself and ran to my cabin. Could my unhooked eyes have been the reason the women were smiling?

Only in part. When I glanced in the mirror before heading back to the meeting, I gasped. What was wrong with my left eye? I could hardly see it.

I leaned into my reflection and smiled. I had forgotten to apply makeup to one eye. The right one sparkled and shone with a touch of gray eye shadow, blue liner, and eyelash-lengthening mascara. But the left one seemed to fade into my face.

In my hurry to make an impression, I had given myself a terrific object lesson: I was so busy promoting "I" that my left "eye" and my hooks and "eyes" were used to show me who "I" really am—an ordinary woman in constant need of God's grace.

All who agree, say "aye."

## Hey, Partner:

It is only natural that you and I feel a sense of pride as we see those pounds melt away. After all, to lose weight is one of the most difficult one-man jobs there is. We have worked long and hard to learn new eating habits, and we like our efforts to be recognized. But we need to be on guard against the pr"I"de that lifts self into the place reserved for the Lord. There's a difference between a healthy sense of accomplishment and the ego-inflating attitude of "I did it and am I good." (And maybe a little better than you.)

That kind of thinking can be even more destructive than our overweight bodies. Pride not only separates us from the people we want to love us but it also separates us from God: ". . . I hate pride and arrogance . ." (Proverbs 8:13b).

As we practice the skills of weight loss, we must continually recognize who our source of life and strength is. One way to do that is to reevaluate our purpose for losing weight. If we are concerned only about others' opinions or promoting ourselves, our resolve to keep the weight off will fade much as my eye did that day. We need to improve our depth of vision by committing ourselves, our food plans, and our ultimate weight loss to the Lord. Only as we depend daily upon His gracious support will we be able to balance the new way we feel about our bodies.

Turn your "eyes—I's—ayes" upon Jesus.

## Clue:

> I looked into the mirror,
> And what did I see?
> Only one eye
> Staring back at me.

## Diet Data:

Don't think you have to give up some of your favorites, such as Stroganoff or cheesecake, just because you are losing weight. Use leaner cuts of meat, yogurt, skim milk, and low-fat creams. You can also cut calories by eating smaller portions and cooking in nonstick pans. One of the best investments you can make to ensure steady weight loss, then maintenance when you reach your goal, is a good low-fat cookbook.

## Solution:

> Now I, Nebuchadnezzar, praise and exalt and glorify the King of heaven, because everything he does is right and all his ways are just. And those who walk in pride he is able to humble.
>
> Daniel 4:37

How do I honestly feel about my weight loss at this point?

Do I compare myself in a negative or positive way with others?

How can either of the above comparisons sabotage my progress?

The "world system" applauds pride. Why is pride offensive to God?

Think of at least one way God has humbled me in the past and write it down.

Now thank Him!

# Paperwork
## (Humor)

### Evidence:

I alluded to this next item of evidence earlier and thought I should give you the whole scoop.

Les and I were guests at Fran's dinner party. I always looked forward to her gourmet meals, for she not only set an elegant table, she also invited the most interesting people. I sat between a neurosurgeon and a magazine publisher, and as I devoured the Boeuf bourguignon, I also ate up every word of my dinner companions.

Then came dessert: a cloud-light lemon chiffon pie set on a lacy paper doily. I couldn't possibly bypass that.

The publisher mentioned my writing (I thought he'd never ask). As I embarked on my literary interest while partaking of the luscious offering before me, I was only moderately aware that Fran's piecrust wasn't up to par. *Oh, well,* I thought, *she's only human, after all.*

I noticed the publisher didn't seem to be listening to my monologue. Instead, he stared at the table in front of me, a smile playing at the corners of his mouth. Why was he smiling at my tale of endless rejection slips? Finally I stopped eating and talking long enough to follow his eyes to my plate.

Only the outside edges of the lacy doily decorated the dark-blue china. What had happened to the center? As I gasped at the realization of what I'd done, all eyes focused on me. No wonder the crust tasted like paper. I had eaten the doily!

## Hey, Partner:

I learned some lessons from that experience: I shouldn't become so enamored of my own words that I lose track of what I'm eating. I shouldn't judge the cook—I might be eating the plate. Most important, I hope I've learned not to take myself so seriously. At first, I was embarrassed to have devoured the doily, but when I realized the humor of the situation, I was able to laugh along with everyone else.

If we can accept ourselves—our foibles and our seeming rejections—with understanding, patience, and a sense of humor, we might avoid a bad case of ulcers or loss of self-esteem. After all, we are *all* only human. I'm not perfect, but neither was the neurosurgeon or the publisher. You know, after that incident, the party came to life as each person related a similar faux pas from his or her own past.

I have found that a sense of humor has saved me from depression on many occasions. Why do we take ourselves so seriously? Perhaps one of the reasons we have weight problems is that we haven't taken time to see the humor in life. If the baby paints the wall with peanut butter, we don't need to salve the situation with a sandwich. Instead, let's make an effort to see the light side of life.

Doctors and psychologists have discovered the healing properties of laughter. As we laugh, tensions are released and our bodies aren't so prone to stress-related diseases. If we see little humor in our own lives, we need to visit someone with children—or perhaps begin to help out in the nursery of the Sunday school. The innocent words and actions of two- and three-year-olds will always bring a smile. Some people enjoy canned humor through a Marx Brothers movie or one of Gary Larson's "Far Side" comic books. There's a ring of truth to that old saying, "Laugh and the world laughs with you, weep and you weep alone."

The most sought-after people I know aren't the ones who wear long faces and produce an instant tale of woe. They are the ones who are able to laugh at circumstances and at themselves. Let's give it a try today. Instead of focusing our frowns on frustrations, let's set our smiles on satisfactions.

Ella Wheeler Wilcox wrote:

> Tis easy enough to be pleasant,
> When life flows along like a song;
> But the man worth while is the one who will smile
> When everything goes dead wrong.

## Clue:

> It didn't hurt my diet,
> For it wasn't even oily.
> There's not a gram of fat
> In a pretty paper doily!

## Diet Data:

Eating is social, but social eating can sabotage your new and improved plan of weight management. Before arriving at a dinner party, decide ahead of time what foods you will allow yourself. If there is an irresistible potato dish, let the bread plate pass by. If the hostess would be offended by a turndown on dessert, eat only a few bites (no doilies). You can excuse yourself: "The rest of the dinner was so delicious, I'm afraid I can't eat such a generous serving of dessert."

If you can't control the amount of food (or decorations) you eat, don't give up your diet—or your social life. Pat yourself on the back for your many successes, and continue on the road to your ultimate weight goal.

## Solution:

> Our mouths were filled with laughter,
>   our tongues with songs of joy.
> Then it was said among the nations,
>   "The Lord has done great things for them."
>
> Psalm 126:2

What type of humor touches my funny bone?


Am I more prone to laugh at subtle humor or slapstick?


When was the last time I laughed at myself? Recall the setting and how I felt.

Do I laugh at myself to cover up insecurity, or am I truly amused? Dig deep for this one.

Are fat people really jolly or more sensitive to painful emotions?

What is the difference between a sense of humor and hiding behind laughter?

# Parole Violations
## (Plateaus)

## Evidence:

Les was on vacation last week, so it seemed a good time for me to be on vacation from my diet, too. *I've done pretty well over the past few months*, I told myself. Sure, I slipped up a few times and the weight wasn't coming off as quickly as I had hoped, but I had only about ten more pounds to lose. I deserved a break!

We began our vacation with a trip to the state fair. I was sure to find all kinds of delicious offerings there and could hardly wait until lunchtime. As I looked over the menu, I decided on the most appetizing of all the sandwiches: breast of turkey.

The rest of the day passed quickly as we took in the exhibits and entertainment. By the time we reached the exit gate, we were too tired to think about stopping for ice cream, so we headed for home.

The next four days we traveled winding roads through ghost towns and national parks, stopping for breakfast, lunch, and dinner at cafés, inns, and McDonald's.

I had every intention of violating my parole in order to enjoy some of the restricted foods I had given up. Why shouldn't I? I felt discouraged. At my last weigh-in, the scale hadn't budged an ounce. In fact, for the last three weeks, I had remained ten pounds from my goal. The lecturer explained the plateau principle: the closer one gets to goal, the slower the weight loss. She said I would have to be even more determined to rid my body of those remaining bulges.

But I wasn't having any of it. While on vacation, I gave myself a parole from meetings, measures, and menus. However, I found myself behaving strangely whenever I had to make a food choice. Greasy hamburgers didn't appeal to me. Neither did hot dogs, potato chips, or chocolate cheesecake. Without exception, after surveying the menu, I requested the very food items I thought I would forsake: salads, turkey, fish, fruit, vegetables. Maybe, just maybe, after all those months, my habits were really changing.

I would get past this plateau in spite of myself.

## Hey, Partner:

Do you have a vacation coming up? Do you always gain five or ten pounds when you are away from home? You don't have to. It might be easier than you think to lose weight while traveling. There isn't a refrigerator door to contend with. You don't have to prepare foods for the family. If you're on the road, it's easy to restrict your eating to three meals a day. No late-night snacks, no seconds.

Vacation time doesn't have to violate our parole. Even

though we have time off from the usual daily schedule, we don't have to revert to bad eating habits. Let's enjoy God's creative handiwork, try another variation of the healthful food we know is good for us, and relax with our traveling companion.

Here's the result of my vacation: I lost two pounds! Can you believe it? When I shared my success with my diet group, I found I wasn't alone. Almost everyone who had been on vacation had actually lost weight.

Just as those winding roads eventually led to places of beauty and rest, so the long road of weight management will finally bring us to thinness and health. Plateaus in dieting as well as in our spiritual lives are inevitable. The hot, dry road must be traveled in order to reach the high places. Don't give up now.

## Clue:

Our problems and circumstances
Can really keep us stressed.
But even in the midst of trouble,
God can give us rest.

## Diet Data:

There are several ways to cut calories while traveling: Ask for salad dressing on the side, then dip the fork tines in the dressing before spearing the vegetables. You get the taste of the dressing without ruining your figure. Ask the waitress about substitutions and deletions such as extra vegetables instead of a baked potato, salad instead of creamy soup, no mayonnaise on the sandwich. Most restaurants are more than happy to oblige. All you need to do is ask.

## Solution:

Then, because so many people were coming and going that they did not even have a chance to eat, [Jesus] said to them, "Come with me by yourselves to a quiet place and get some rest."

Mark 6:31

If I have yet to reach a weight plateau, how will I react when I get there?

Do I think of vacation as a time to violate parole? Why? Why not?

How have my eating choices changed since beginning my weight-loss program?

Have I reached a plateau in my spiritual life where I'm no longer growing as a Christian?

What will I do to continue my spiritual journey?

What Solution to stress did Jesus offer? How will I respond?

Am I stressed or at rest? Explain.

# The Ten Most Unwanted
## (Irrational Thoughts)

## Evidence:

I so wanted to impress my new in-laws the first time they came to dinner, but as a young bride my repertoire of recipes was limited. I could prepare pork chops, toss a tuna casserole, and simmer a spaghetti sauce. I decided to go with the pasta and pesto, and for an encore, I built a blueberry pie—my first.

My husband's mother was an expert pie baker, and choosing such a creation revealed my inexperience—and false confidence.

"What's this?" my husband asked, peering at the brownish disk on the kitchen counter.

"It's your favorite," I beamed, slicing triangles of the thick crust to be presented to our waiting guests. "Blueberry pie."

"But," he drawled, staring at the thin purple line dividing the crusts, "where are the blueberries?"

"I guess I should have used the whole can of berries," I explained to my patient in-laws as they graciously ate the tinted crust.

I decided I was a failure at cooking and turned my attention to cultivating houseplants. But my greenhousewifery wilted. The split-leaf philodendron split down the middle, the spider plant crawled back into its web, and the asparagus fern soon became a candidate for hollandaise sauce. I don't know what I did wrong. The book said watering the plants too much would turn the leaves yellow and not enough would turn them brown. Nothing was said about black or white leaves.

I tried sewing and knitting, but my children refused to wear skirts with upside-down zippers, and my husband said there was no way that third sleeve on his sweater could pass as a cowl collar.

My attempt at painting the front of the house with water-based paint was a washout, and my wallpapering project was no more than a sticky situation. So I turned to food for comfort and satisfaction. Now, as I'm learning new eating habits and relying more on the Lord instead of on a full stomach, at last I'm getting back in touch with my feelings. And as I do, I let go of some of my misbeliefs and irrational thoughts about myself. I'm beginning to try new things again—and in the process, I'm finding I can succeed. After all, if I can lose weight, I can do anything else I really want to.

## Hey, Partner:

God has given each one of us abilities with which to serve Him. Unfortunately, we may have become sidetracked along the path of life when our attempts seemed to fail. If those we love and depend on neglect to supply the strokes we need, we may handcuff ourselves with a list of irrational thoughts.

Those beliefs can not only make us miserable, they also can drive us to food or some other self-destructive addiction. I've come up with ten most unwanted thoughts that are certain to lock up my creativity. Are some of them yours, too? Look them over and pinpoint those you have adopted. Then we'll find a key to unlock these bonds, one by one.

1. I can't do anything right.
2. I don't have any talents.
3. I can't say no.
4. I have to please everybody.
5. I don't have the advantages others do.
6. No one understands me.
7. I can't take criticism.
8. Others expect too much of me.
9. I am shy.
10. God couldn't really love me as I am.

I'm sure you could add to this list, but these illogical beliefs about ourselves are enough to cripple us for a lifetime. However, we can get a reprieve. There is no need to be in bondage to "The Ten Most Unwanted."

Now, partner, it's time for you to do some digging on your own. I'll supply the combination, but you get to open up the safe deposit box of God's Word. In the Bible, you'll find a key to each one of these ten most unwanted thoughts. Please don't skip by this portion of today's entry. Take all the time you need to plumb the depths of these rich words. They may be the most valuable discoveries you find in this book. Ready?

1. Check out Philippians 4:13 to see that you *can do everything.*
2. See 1 Corinthians 12:7–11 for God's specialized gift list.
3. James 4:7 gives the key to being able to say no.

4. Even Jesus, the Son of God, was not loved by everyone. Unlock this thought with John 15:18–21.

5. God's Word shows how to be free from this misbelief in 1 Timothy 6:6–10.

6. God not only understood Solomon's heart, He also understands every thought and motive of everyone: 1 Chronicles 28:9.

7. It isn't too hard to take criticism with this key: 2 Corinthians 12:10.

8. Look back at 2 Corinthians 12:9 to find strength for whatever task needs doing.

9. Jeremiah found the answer to shyness in Jeremiah 1:6–9.

10. God's Word refutes this irrational thought throughout both the Old and New Testaments. What more can He do to prove His love for us than what we read in Romans 5:8?

Now that we know "The Ten Most Unwanted," we no longer need to fear them.

We can be free!

# Clue:

As we think, so we are,
Is what the Bible says.
When I exchange the bad for good,
My thoughts are filled with praise.

# Diet Data:

Now might be a good time to go through the cupboards again to see if any of your personal ten most unwanted foods have somehow found a space on the shelf. Remember those trigger foods that shoot holes in your resolve?

(Oh-oh, how did that chunky peanut butter get back in there?)

## Solution:

> For though we live in the world, we do not wage war as the world does. The weapons we fight with are not the weapons of the world. On the contrary, they have divine power to demolish strongholds. We demolish arguments and every pretension that sets itself up against the knowledge of God, and we take captive every thought to make it obedient to Christ.
>
> 2 Corinthians 10:3–5

171

Which of the ten most unwanted thoughts hold me in their grip? Choose the most prevalent one.

Write out the Scripture reference that applies to this thought.

Memorize this Scripture verse by repeating it several times a day.

When I begin to feel the release from one thought, I will then begin to unlock the next one that binds me. What is it?

List any other irrational thoughts that keep me from a life of freedom.

"If the Son sets you free, you will be free indeed" (John 8:36).

# Trial and Error
## (Learn From Mistakes)

## Evidence:

I have been called for jury duty about five times, yet I've never served as a member. It isn't that I don't want to participate in the trial process, but so far I haven't been among the chosen. Twice the jurors were selected before I had a turn to answer the attorneys' questions; twice I had read too much about the cases and therefore was disqualified; and the last time I knew some of the people involved, so I was dismissed.

I have to be honest (isn't that something a juror must swear to?), but I do have a difficult time presuming a person innocent until proven guilty. That is especially difficult when the police testify to finding this person at the scene of the crime not only with a smoking gun in his hand but also with his pockets full of drugs. Yet I believe in the system. Suppose the

173

defendant had simply been walking by when the crime was perpetrated and the criminal knocked him down, put the gun in his hand, and stuffed his pockets with drugs. Wouldn't that person deserve a fair trial? An unbiased jury?

I've come to the place in *Murder on the FAT Express* where I have to sit back and listen to the evidence. Did I murder FAT? Have I been guilty of judging myself too harshly? Do I know all the facts about the case? As I reach the weight goal I have set for myself, has my success been the result of trial and error, or have I learned enough to maintain an ideal weight for the rest of my life?

I know I've made many mistakes in judgment over these past months. There were times when my food choice wasn't a mistake but simply a rebellion against the diet process. I deliberately sabotaged my efforts. There were nights when I anguished over my weakness and hated myself for overeating—again. I often had to face my food addiction before the Lord, receive His forgiveness, then forgive myself before I could go on. Yes, there has been an abundance of errors, but as I put my efforts on trial today, I thank the Lord for His grace in enabling me to presume my innocence until proven guilty.

Almost there. Only a few more pounds to go. I feel a little scared. A little apprehensive. A little intimidated. But the prosecutor (Satan) has no power over my Judge. His words are lies, and I don't need to be afraid of the future. Jesus is my defense. He will present my case, then see me through to the end.

On with the trial!

## Hey, Partner:

I don't know where you are today in your efforts to murder FAT, but whether you have reached your goal or still have months of calorie counting ahead of you, don't make any plea bargains. You are doing what is right for you. Your body is already more energetic, and your esteem has grown with every lost pound.

You may have read through this book in one sitting and are now ready to take a day at a time and work out the questions. I hope, for your own growth and satisfaction, that you won't skip over the self-evaluations. Last night I read them over again and learned some new things about myself that I hadn't yet explored—or admitted.

Our overweight has become a problem (even if it is only a few pounds) that can deplete our creative energy, clog our arteries, and depress our emotions. We feel trapped, hopeless, and sometimes desperate. But as we carefully and prayerfully go through the questions at the end of each entry, we will discover *why* we are overweight and *how* to overcome that oppressor: FAT. We will be real-life detectives! Our spiritual nature will grow when we exercise faith in the Scripture portions; and though we may never again have skinny teenage bodies, we will have greater health and the freedom to think about something other than food.

If you have gone through this book on a daily basis, answered all the questions, and still have weight to lose, start from the beginning again. Read your answers over and add to them as your insights deepen. You are going to make it this time.

You are a victor—not a victim!

# Clue:

Overruled or sustained?
Which shall it be,
When the prosecutor shouts, "Guilty!"
And points his finger at me.

## Diet Data:

Keep up the exercise! Professionals say the steady movement of regular exercise will not only cause the fat to leave the adipose tissue where it is stored but the fat will also be shuttled off to the bloodstream and to the liver, where it is burned. Fat lost only through dieting with no exercise will simply recirculate in the blood and find its way back to the hips and thighs.

## Solution:

For there is one God and one mediator between God and men, the man Christ Jesus, who gave himself as a ransom for all men—the testimony given in its proper time.

1 Timothy 2:5,6

Has my weight loss been the result of trial and error, or have I built a strong case?

How many more pounds do I need to lose to reach my goal weight?

What three things have I learned about myself that added to my weight problem?

How have I changed (or how am I going to change) my actions in order to lose weight permanently?

Write a paragraph expressing how I feel about myself right now and what my expectations are for the days and months ahead.

Commit those feelings and hopes to my Defense Attorney, the one Mediator between myself and God: Jesus Christ.

Case Dismissed!

# Verdict: Not Guilty!
## (Goal)

## Evidence:

It was a dark and stormy night. . . .

Actually it is a bright, sunny morning—the morning I will at last see my goal weight on the scale!

I'm ready to write the last chapter of this mystery story, *Murder on the FAT Express*. It has taken months of surveillance, night watches, grilling suspects, and intense detective work. But the mystery has been solved, the suspects have been arrested, the defendant has been tried, and the jury has reached a decision.

As I approach my Saturday-morning appointment with the group that has been my support over these past months, I think back to the first morning I walked—no, slouched—into that room of enthusiastic men and women. I had struggled with the decision to murder FAT and had finally gathered all my determination to sign my name on the dotted line. That had been one of the best, though hardest, decisions I had made in several years.

This morning I feel like a new person as I breeze into the meeting place. My slim shadow is not an optical illusion this time, for over the days, weeks, months, and seasons I have left behind that big-as-a-barn shadow. I'm not wearing a loose topper that grazes my knees or pants with an elastic band. Today, after I tucked in a bright-red shirt, I zipped up a pair of jeans and fashion-modeled them in front of my wide-eyed husband.

"You look great, honey," he said, wrapping his arms around me. (He does that a lot these days.) "I'm so proud of you."

"Me, too," I admitted. "But even more than that, I just feel so good! I can breathe comfortably now. I can walk faster, work longer, and I feel so happy!" I paused to thank the Lord for His constant grace, then added, "I don't ever want to be fat again."

Now as I walk into the meeting, I'm greeted by friends who reached their goal before I did and friends who have weeks, even months, to go. And there are always the new friends, people who feel the way I did those many months ago: Desperate. Hopeful.

I step on the scale. The cute, slim, bright-eyed leader smiles her beautiful smile. "You did it!" she proclaims. "You have reached your goal. Congratulations!"

I sit among my peers, a smile reaching from one ear to the other. We encourage the new ones, compliment the older ones, and express our gratitude for all the help and support we have received from one another.

But now what?

As I leave the group, get back into my car, and drive home, I make a commitment to the Lord, to myself, and to all the people who have helped me: I will continue to practice what I've learned. I will continue to be in touch with the emotions that drove me to overeating. I will live one day at a time.

. . . and they lived happily ever after.

# Hey, Partner:

The jury is in and ready to announce its decision. They had reams of evidence to consider, pros and cons to weigh, and now the judge asks for the verdict.

"We the members of the jury find the defendant not guilty. The murder of FAT was not a matter of premeditated revenge on the victim's body. It was purely an act of self-defense."

Hurray! We did it, partner. We didn't cut off a life when we murdered FAT; we cut away death. Our arteries are healthier now that we have changed our eating habits, our hearts don't have to work so hard to pump blood through those extra miles of veins, and possibly we have added years—enjoyable years—to our life spans.

We have, with the help of inside and outside sources, solved the mystery of our compulsive food addiction. Does this mean we no longer have to contend with decisions of what or what not to eat? Are we free to eat whatever and whenever we want now, no longer restricted by the rules and regulations that brought us to this happy state?

I would love to be able to believe that from now on you and I could eat like normal people. But just as a man or woman who is born into God's family must still bear his old nature along with the new nature of Christ's indwelling Spirit, we must continue to control that old drive to overeat when we feel threatened, lonely, frustrated, or bored.

But we're not alone. We still have the Lord and His Book of Solutions to help us. We have murdered FAT. Now, with patience and perseverance, we can see to it that FAT stays where it belongs: in the grave.

# Clue:

In the grave
Is where FAT should be,
Not in the gravy,
Where it can get back on me!

# Diet Data:

Slowly add one or two of your trigger foods back into your diet. Try *one* scoop of ice cream for a Friday night treat. You might also have a peanut butter sandwich on Wednesday afternoon. But take it easy. Continue to weigh on the same day each week. Watch the numbers on the scale. If they fluctuate too much, adjust your eating program. It will take several months for you to know how many calories your new weight needs for maintenance. Be patient with yourself and enjoy the freedom you have to slip into a pair of slacks or zip up a dress without the misery of unwanted bulges.

# Solution:

Let us draw near to God with a sincere heart in full assurance of faith, having our hearts sprinkled to cleanse us from a guilty conscience and having our bodies washed with pure water.

Hebrews 10:22

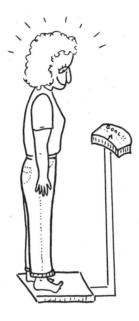

Now that I have reached my goal, how do I feel about myself?

As I look to the future, am I fearful or faithful? Why?

Write a positive statement about my new body.

From 1 to 10, list interests such as hobbies and/or service opportunities I can do instead of filling up my time with eating or negative woolgathering.

1.

2.

3.

4.

5.

6.

7.

8.

9.

10.

Record my goal weight here_____

One week later_____

Two weeks later_____

Three weeks later_____

Four weeks later_____